Intelligent Leadership

Intelligent Leadership

Creating a passion for change

Alan Hooper
and
John Potter

RANDOM HOUSE
BUSINESS BOOKS

Alan Hooper and John Potter have asserted their rights under the Copyright, Designs and Patents Act, 1988, to be identified as the authors of this work.

First published in 2000 by Random House Business Books,
The Random House Group Limited,
20 Vauxhall Bridge Road, London SW1V 2SA

Random House Australia (Pty) Limited
20 Alfred Street, Milsons Point,
Sydney, New South Wales 2061, Australia

Random House New Zealand Limited
18 Poland Road, Glenfield,
Auckland 10, New Zealand

Random House (Pty) Limited
Endulini, 5a Jubilee Road, Parktown 2193, South Africa

The Random House Group Limited Reg. No. 954009

Papers used by The Random House Group Limited
are natural, recyclable products made from wood grown in
sustainable forests. The manufacturing processes conform to
the environmental regulations of the country of origin.

ISBN 0 7126 8415 8

Companies, institutions and other organisations wishing to make
bulk purchases of books published by Random House should
contact their local bookstore or Random House direct:
Special Sales Director
Random House, 20 Vauxhall Bridge Road, London SW1V 2SA
Tel 020 7840 8470   Fax 020 7828 6681

www.randomhouse.co.uk
businessbooks@randomhouse.co.uk

Typeset by MATS, Southend-on-Sea, Essex
Printed and bound in the United Kingdom by
Biddles Ltd, Guildford and King's Lynn

Contents

FOREWORD

In a day gone by, running an organization seemed akin to conducting a symphony orchestra. Nowadays, I think it's more like leading a jazz ensemble. There's more improvisation. Someone once wrote that the sound of surprise is jazz, and if there is anything we need to cultivate a taste for in this world, it's surprise, the unexpected, the unimaginable. In essence, we need to acquire a taste for change.

That is precisely what Alan Hooper and John Potter help us to do in *Intelligent Leadership*. The book makes it plain that the best kind of change one could hope to bring to any organization is a receptivity to further change. It explores a range of significant related issues. What do ordinary women and men have at stake? What hidden motivations hinder or encourage change? Beyond examining the internal and external forces of change themselves, Alan and John do an estimable job of addressing the often-overlooked human themes related to change – the emotional and psychological aspects.

Cataclysmic shifts affect the business world more quickly than other families of organizations, thanks to our global economy. A successful business leader is like an early pioneer of the American frontier, waking up each morning to new terrain and new adventures. The words of Walt Whitman come to mind: 'We must bear the brunt of danger, we the youthful sinewy races, all the rest on us depend, Pioneers!' Nurturing a frontier spirit is an important element of acquiring a taste for change.

Over the course of the years, I've been increasingly convinced that good leadership is ultimately grounded in good character. This book offers an insightful look at the issue at the organizational level. Alan and John note that a yawning chasm often separates an organization's vision statement from its established culture, but also note that successful ones – the ones that can hope to create a 'passion for change' – have strong and consistent values that permeate every level of those organizations.

Chapter Seven examines the imperative to remain strategic, to hold a compass firmly in our grasp while moving through the thick mist. In the face of constant uncertainty, many persons in positions of authority respond with either a fatalistic attitude or a rigid, controlling approach. 'Intelligent leadership' involves abandoning both fatalism and rigid control in order to explore the creative possibilities implied in each new moment. As always, the challenge is for change to serve people rather than for people to serve as puppets of change.

It is an essentially human trait to try to understand and predict the future. The future is for me a portmanteau word, one that embraces a number of notions. First, it involves an exercise in imagination which allows us to compete with and try to outwit events that lie ahead. Second, the attempt to shape what is to come is a social invention that legitimizes the process of strategic planning. There is no other way to resist the 'tyranny of blind forces' than by looking circumstances in the face – as we experience them in the present – and extrapolating how they may unfold, nor is there any better way to detect a compromise of a leader's or an organization's goals or values.

Organizational plans for change all too often serve narrow, short-term priorities while forgetting to ask overarching questions that determine the quality of all our lives – questions such as: Is this right? Is it good for our children? Is it good for the planet? 'Intelligent leadership' factors in societal obligations as well as institutional ones in the course of its planning.

Over the years I have given executives, public servants and others advice on how best to lead, offering such insights as the necessity of leading as opposed to simply managing. But perhaps the most durable counsel I can give leaders is to stay nimble. More than ever, leaders must prepare for what has not yet been imagined, in order to bring order out of chaos. Having in recent decades witnessed the beginnings of one revolution after another (the information explosion is only one), it's become clear that change is the only constant and will remain so for who knows how long.

Finally, while change, as Machiavelli noted, has no constituency, it is the fundamental task of today's and tomorrow's leaders to establish constituencies, by fostering an environment that embraces inexorable change as an opportunity. In that sense, organizations can hope to be like the jazz quartet that loves the unexpected and would have it no other way. Alan and John write that 'it is important to have fun.' I believe *Intelligent Leadership* will help leaders and those they serve to do just that in these turbulent times.

Warren Bennis
University of Southern California

MOVING FORWARDS

The people we interviewed for this book were in the appointments quoted at the time of writing. Several have already moved on to new appointments whilst the book has been in production. We apologise for any inconvenience this may cause the reader – it is simply a feature of our rapidly changing times.

ACKNOWLEDGEMENTS

The writing of any book involves many heroes. In particular, the Centre for Leadership Studies at the University of Exeter has provided us with an excellent background for the research undertaken for this book.

We owe a great debt to all those excellent leaders who have very kindly allowed us to interview them about their experiences, thus providing us with primary research material. There are also the clients with whom we have worked over the past ten years including ABIN, Barclays Bank, Eli Lilly, GKN Westland Helicopters, Lloyds Bank, Nationwide Building Society, NatWest Bank, Sony UK, South-West Water, Watts Blake Bearne and The Wrigley Company. The Public Sector has also supported our efforts to uncover the secrets of successful change leadership. In particular, the National Health Service, Somerset County Council and various city and district councils have all played their part. The Armed Services have also welcomed us both back as occasional visitors even after we had chosen to desert them for the worlds of consulting and academia!

Any list of thanks, inevitably, is incomplete but we would like to mention the following: John Adair, Mair Barnes, Bob Baty, Meredith Belbin, Warren Bennis, Richard Benson, Goran Carstedt, Sir Paul Condon, Sir Peter Davis, Ekow Eshun, Tony Everett, Lino Formica, Arie de Geus, Charles Handy, Sir Stuart Hampson, Sir Geoffrey Holland, Richard Ide, Ken Keir, John Kotter, Graham Lawson, Leo McKee, Tim Melville-Ross, Jim Mowatt, Brand Pretorius, Gail Rebuck, John Roberts, Philip Sadler, Edgar Schein and Tony Stables.

Although we have tried to acknowledge the sources of as many of our thoughts as possible, we have undoubtedly missed some of them and we apologise for any oversights in that respect. We do have an excuse – as time passes by, good ideas often merge into common sense and we often forget their origins.

There are also the dedicated people at Random House such as Simon Wilson, Clare Smith and, of course, Gail Rebuck who acted as our sponsor for this book.

Finally, and most important of all, we thank our wives Jan and Marjorie for their ideas, patience and understanding whilst we have been writing this book together. Without their support, we would have found life very difficult.

Alan Hooper
John Potter
January 2000

Special note:

The subject of political correctness is one we take seriously. The history of leadership is dogged with the tag of 'male, military and Western', and we hope that the reader will soon realise that this is far from the way we see leadership. In the text we have tried to use 'she' or 'he' alternately, talking in terms of 'she/he' or 'he/she'. No bias is implied. This issue becomes very relevant when using military language. Units are often referred to as 'a four-man cell'. In the modern world this can just as often be 'a four-woman cell' or 'a four-person cell'. However, to fit in to the common language which is understood by the majority we occasionally do use the male descriptor. No bias is implied and we are firmly of the belief that both women and men are equally capable of creating outstandingly effective leadership processes in their organisations. We have become even more convinced of this during our interviews when we have noticed the increasing number of women successfully holding senior management and leadership positions in both the public and private sectors.

LIST OF FIGURES

LIST OF TABLES

Appetiser

CHAPTER ONE

In this chapter, you will:

- **COME TO REALISE THAT CHANGE IS OFTEN SEEN AS A THREAT RATHER THAN A CHALLENGE BECAUSE OF THE WAY IT IS HANDLED IN ORGANISATIONS**

- **REALISE THAT PEOPLE CAN LEARN TO LOVE CHANGE – THEY JUST DON'T LIKE TO BE CHANGED**

- **HAVE A GLIMPSE OF THE FUTURE OF WORK**

- **SEE HOW LEADERSHIP FITS IN TO THE PATTERN OF CHANGE**

- **START TO THINK ABOUT WHAT IT MEANS TO BE A 'LEARNING LEADER'**

- **BEGIN TO THINK OF LEADERSHIP AS AN EMOTIONAL PROCESS THAT LEADS TO THE IDEA OF 'INTELLIGENT LEADERSHIP'**

- **START TO REALISE THAT LEADERSHIP IS MORE ABOUT PERSUASION AND UNLOCKING HUMAN POTENTIAL THAN IT IS ABOUT COMMAND AND CONTROL**

- **GAIN AN OVERVIEW OF THE REST OF THIS BOOK.**

Why This Book?

Change. The very word inspires such a wide variety of responses that it is difficult to know where to begin. Most of our organisations are inept at leading and implementing change – every day throughout the civilised countries of the world we see the results of this lack of ability. Work-related stress, political battles in the boardroom, endless struggles to maintain and develop individual power bases and the problems of employee dis-illusionment are rife in many companies and public-sector organisations. In too many jobs, employees at all levels feel that they are in a socially toxic environment, where to take a risk and innovate is to dice with death, if only in career terms! The consequence is that people feel stifled, unappreciated and become resigned to working in the same old ineffective ways.

At the same time, they fear change because, usually, it means the threat of loss. Loss of colleagues, of familiar working practices, of routines, of predictability and even of employment. 'Rightsizing', 'downsizing', 'out-sourcing', 'rightsourcing' and the other business expressions of the current time all appear to be geared to the idea that organisations seem to squeeze the last drop of work out of their employees. The concern is that once organisations have done this, then they will consign their people to the scrap heap, often in their mid-forties, to make way for the new generation (usually university graduates), all of whom are less expensive to employ, will work harder to finance their first mortgages and family commitments, and who will contribute endless ideas and creativity in the name of 'career advancement'.

Rosabeth Moss Kanter[1] points out the ineptitude of many organisations in handling the change issue and Table 1.1 highlights some of the frequent mistakes which are made. We have extracted what Kanter calls the rules for stifling innovation and we have seen them occur in many organisational situations.

Table 1.1 *THE NEGATIVE SIDE OF CHANGE*

HOW ORGANISATIONS FREQUENTLY MISHANDLE CHANGE

(*Based on the observations of Rosabeth Moss Kanter and our own*)

How many of these examples are typical of how your organisation handles change? Tick the box on the right of the statement and total your score.

1. Regard any new idea from below with suspicion – because it's new and because it's from below. ☐

2. Insist that people who need your approval to act first go through several other levels of management to get their signatures. ☐

3. Ask departments or individuals to challenge and criticise each other's proposals.
    (That saves you the job of deciding; you just pick the survivor.) ☐

4. Express your criticisms freely, and withhold your praise.
    (That keeps people on their toes.) Let them know how they can be fired at any time. ☐

5. Treat identification of problems as signs of failure, to discourage people from letting you know when something in their area isn't working. ☐

6. Control everything carefully. Make sure people count anything that can be counted, frequently. ☐

7. Make decisions to reorganise or change policies in secret, and spring them on people unexpectedly.
    (That also keeps people on their toes.) ☐

8. Make sure that requests for information are fully justified, and make sure that it is not given out to managers freely.
    (You don't want data to fall into the wrong hands.) ☐

9. Assign to lower-level managers, in the name of delegation and participation, responsibility for figuring out how to cut back, lay off, move people around, or otherwise implement threatening decisions you have made.
    And get them to do it quickly. ☐

10. And above all, never forget that you, the higher-ups, already know everything important about this business. ☐

Your 'change screw-up' score out of 10

Is this an overly cynical viewpoint? It may be so. Despite what we have just claimed, many organisations ARE value-driven, DO care about people and ARE concerned with making the workplace a 'good place to be'. So where is the problem with change? Is it not in everyone's benefit to want to improve things, to work more effectively, to outperform the competition and to excel in the market place? The answer is, of course, that change itself can be beneficial to all concerned provided it is handled correctly. It is the mis-management – or mis-leadership – of the change process which causes the problems. In fact we have formed the opinion that human beings can learn to thrive on change. People CAN learn to change – it's just that they don't like to BE changed!

The goal of this book is to help the business leader at whatever level he or she operates to be more effective in handling the change issue, particularly in human terms. We intend creating a marriage of a number of important concepts; those related to leadership and those related to the effective creation and management of change. In this way, we feel we can make a real contribution to the world of work – the world which is based on perceptions rather than fact, on emotion rather than logic.

To the Chief Executive, 'change' means displaying leadership by develop-ing a vision of the future, crafting strategies to bring that vision into reality and then dealing with the crises along the way. It is also about winning political battles to ensure that everybody in the organisation is mobilising their energies towards the same goals and objectives – the process we call 'emotional alignment'.

To the production line worker, the salesperson and the truck driver, change frequently poses a threat to the *status quo*. Just when things seem to have settled into a predictable routine, someone has the idea to bring in some 'change', often for obscure reasons but usually geared towards gaining more work from people for less money. It is easy to be cynical about change. Apart from anything else, it means that inevitably there will be winners and losers. And frequently it is not the people who are 'let go' in a downsizing type of operation who are always the losers. In many cases they move on to better jobs and careers through force of circumstance. What is now emerging is the so-called 'Survivor Syndrome' experienced by those who survive the current round of job losses. And it is these individuals who frequently pose the greatest challenge in human terms to the leadership of our organisations.

■ The increasing challenge of change

There is no doubt that the challenge of change is increasing. As we enter the twenty-first century, we have seen more changes in the way we live, work and carry out our business than for hundreds of years previously. For instance, according to a report commissioned by the Royal Society of Arts in 1996,[2] the changes experienced in the last ten years are irreversible and are having major implications for the future of work. In the UK less than 60% of the workforce is in full-time jobs (and this is declining); 28% of all jobs are part-time; 80-90% of new jobs will go to women; women will account for 55% of employees by the turn of the century; managers work 120 hours a year longer than fifty years ago; and nearly 33% of men and women took their pension by the age of fifty-four.

It is interesting to note the considerable changes that have taken place in the last decade of the twentieth century. We have seen the disappearance of the Berlin Wall, the emergence of the Internet, a virtual explosion in our ability to communicate internationally with mobile telephones, the 'liberation' of South Africa in terms of the abolition of apartheid, and truly global competition in almost every business sector. In some respects, we must agree with Warren Bennis' suggestion that our world has just been in existence for around ten years with regard to the way we live on a daily basis! If the rate of change is increasing, then it is somewhat daunting to think what the next decade might bring.

Perhaps more significant than the changes we have experienced to date are those that are predicted for the future. According to another report commissioned by Barclays Life,[3] going to work in 2020 will be very different from 2000. For a start we will face a number of choices. There will be shorter working hours (due to technology improvements); 25% of us will work from home; many of us may work a three- or four-day week in order to concentrate our working hours. This will free up the extra one or two days to pursue leisure activities or do community work. There will be an enormous increase in computer power, so much so that it is estimated that 'one desktop computer in 2020 will be as powerful as all the computers in Silicon Valley today'. The PC may well develop into a PN – a personal network embracing voice response systems and virtual glasses receiving wireless digital video which will 'enable us to talk and see anybody in the world whilst still on the move'. These extraordinary changes to our lives are the environment in which leaders will have to operate in the future.

In this book, we have set out to examine how leaders, across a broad spectrum, have faced up to and dealt with the challenge of change. We have interviewed a wide variety of individuals in settings ranging from large transnational corporations to small local businesses, from large public-sector services undergoing privatisation to individuals in the educational world faced with a global marketplace in terms of their customers. It has been a fascinating journey. At times we have thought we had the one answer to many of the problems associated with change. However, we ultimately found that not to be true. What we did find, however, were recurrent themes which time and again underpinned the effective change leadership processes we explored.

One of those themes is the importance of behaviour on the part of the leader in shaping both the culture of the organisation and the attitudes of individual employees. Edgar Schein[4] discusses the link between leadership and culture in terms of the leader creating a culture based on surface artefacts, espoused values and basic underlying assumptions. During the past few years expressions such as 'walking the talk', 'managing by walking around', 'leader visibility' and 'values-based' leadership have become commonplace. We have come to the conclusion that effective change leadership is not so much about what the leader says in terms of rhetoric, but rather what they actually DO, particularly in terms of how they deal with people on an individual level. And leaders set the example for creation of the culture of the organisation in terms of the surface level symbols such as dress code, buildings and so forth, together with how they display their true values and underlying assumptions.

Both authors have extensive experience of running strategic leadership sessions for both private and public-sector organisations. These sessions are based on the idea of creating a vision or mission statement which relates to a set of corporate values, of what is important in the way business is conducted. Implicitly, these are based on the underlying assumptions and beliefs of the organisation. In many cases, we have seen this effort totally wasted, because even when the strategic direction is created, the problems arise when top management fails to behave in a way to support their stated value set.

For example, one value that occurs regularly relates to the importance of people. 'People are our most important asset' has a familiar ring about it! However, it is not uncommon for a company to publish this or something similar as part of their values statement one week – and then the following week make a substantial number of people redundant. The reaction from the workforce is a natural one; people believe what they see rather than what they hear. Once one value has been undermined in behavioural terms, the others become suspect and, as a result, the whole 'strategic direction' setting process falls apart in disarray – all because the leadership of the organisation says one thing but does something else, usually driven by short-term thinking.

■ A vested interest

As authors, we have a vested interest in change. Both of us have successfully changed careers during our lives in an attempt to meet the challenges of the unpredictable world around us. Although these transitions were not always comfortable experiences they have taught us that the only way to deal with change is to embrace it and not resist it. And this is the challenge faced by all organisations, certainly the ones we researched. In all, we interviewed some twenty-five leaders in both the public and private sectors. We chose individuals who had both a significant impact on the organisations with which they are involved, and who were also clearly 'learning leaders'.

■ Thought on leadership has progressed

So leadership has to be our start point in understanding how to handle the change issue. As we discuss in Chapter Three, thought on leadership has progressed considerably during the past century. What is now abundantly clear is that effective leadership is a process created by an individual rather than a focus on that individual's personal qualities. This means that no longer can leaders be complacent about their personal abilities to create effective processes in their organisations. The world around us is changing at such a pace that the 'learning leader' concept has to be the way for the future. We have chosen the title Intelligent Leadership for exactly that reason. The ideas of 'brainy leadership' and 'the thinking leader' have been around for some time. What we have done is to explore leadership both in terms of the processes created and also the appropriateness of those processes to given situations.

■ The importance of emotion

In many respects we are of the view that leadership is primarily an emotional process and so we have leaned significantly on the ideas of Daniel Goleman with his concept of Emotional Intelligence.[5] Emotion is being increasingly recognised as having a major impact on how successful we are in coming to terms with the demands made on us by our progress through life. For many years, particularly in the business world, people have fought shy of the word 'emotion' believing it to be counterproductive to the ideas of maintaining control and discipline within organisations. Yet emotion is the very issue that enables us both to maintain control on a personal level and also to create that sense of discipline which is often lacking in so many organisations. We have thus approached this whole subject of effective change leadership from the viewpoint of understanding how successful change leaders master the emotional dimension of change through the behaviours they display. Goleman has identified five areas which underpin the concept of Emotional Intelligence and in many respects these provide a sound footing for understanding effective change leadership. In fact we suggest that these same five areas underpin our concept of 'Intelligent Leadership' because, in the final analysis, leadership is about the emotional impact produced upon the led which transforms their behaviour so that they can reach a higher level of performance.

■ Exploring Intelligent Leadership

The first area of Intelligent Leadership relates to the leader acquiring self-knowledge. 'Know thyself' has been a well-used phrase throughout history and never has it been more relevant than in today's turbulent times. Effective change leaders are aware of their strengths and weaknesses, and capitalise on both their own abilities and those of their colleagues. A key part of self-knowledge is the skill of listening. This is a skill which so many leaders seem to lose towards the end of their reign. For instance, many commentators say that this was the downfall of Margaret Thatcher in the 1990s because, following her successes in the Falklands War and in the creation of an international reputation of the 'Iron Lady', she seemed to develop the idea that she was unassailable and that she could ignore the advice of her cabinet. This ultimately led to her downfall and provides a useful lesson for all leaders, whatever their sphere of activity.

Managing emotions is the second of Goleman's Emotional Intelligence issues and this translates in leadership terms into managing morale, both on the part of the leader and the led. In our earlier book *The Business of Leadership*[6] we suggested seven basic Leadership Competencies, the seventh of which is decision-making in crisis. It seems a vital part of effective leadership, particularly in times of change, that the leader can handle his or her emotions as well as those of the followers. The issue of 'morale' has always figured high on the leadership agenda, and this is an even more important aspect of leadership in handling change.

The other six competencies are: setting direction, setting an example, effective communication, creating alignment, bringing the best out of people and acting as a change agent. These are explored further in Chapter Three.

Our fourth competency (alignment) relates to the third element of Emotional Intelligence, the harnessing of emotions. In all change situations, one of the most important aspects is managing human energy and ensuring that everyone is working towards a common aim. Thus emotional alignment means channelling as much human energy as possible towards bringing the vision into reality – and not wasting it in internal conflict.

One aspect of change which frequently needs consideration is the idea of the critical mass. This is the body of individuals who have to be won over, emotionally at least, to the new ideas and ways of working. Emotional alignment is a key issue in terms of harnessing emotions.

■ The Leader as Persuader not Controller

Understanding others and their viewpoint is a key element of both Emotional Intelligence and Intelligent Leadership. Jay Conger has already pointed towards the idea of 'Persuasive Leadership' in an article,[7] published in the *Harvard Business Review*. Empathy and the understanding of the viewpoint of the followers is a key factor in Intelligent Leadership which persuades rather than coerces followers. We will look into Conger's approach to Persuasive Leadership in a little more detail later in the book.

The final element of Emotional Intelligence which translates directly to Intelligent Leadership is that of relationship management. The successful management of relationships is vital for both organisations and individuals. In general, the corporate world now recognises that effective relationship management does not just apply to customers but to other stakeholders as well, including employees, shareholders, suppliers and the community at large. Successful, intelligent leaders in the future must remember that they, too, have

a range of 'stakeholders' as far their operation is concerned, not just followers.

■ A practical approach

As we move forward to starting our journey into effective change leadership using the perspectives of both Emotional Intelligence and Intelligent Leadership, it is important to realise that the purpose of this book is to be a practical tool for helping leaders at all levels to be more effective in the way that they handle the issues of change. Whilst we will present some theoretical and conceptual tools which really do help manage and implement change more effectively, we believe that the main value in this book lies in the interviews we have undertaken. We carried out structured interviews with some twenty-five individuals who had reputations for being effective change leaders. We chose our respondents carefully and they represent a wide range of organisational settings, drawn both from the private and the public sector. They also represent a range of geographical settings. We have talked with leaders in Europe, South Africa and the United States of America, as well as in the United Kingdom.

Our respondents all displayed considerable leadership both in terms of the tasks they were undertaking and how they dealt with the people involved. It became clear that they had developed a natural feel for effective leadership, even if they had not read all the books on the subject! Good ideas and practices tend to emerge from experience, be that experience good or bad. In this book we have set out to help the reader shortcircuit the bad experiences by learning from others. As a result, it should help leaders and managers at all levels to operate more effectively. One thing that all leaders seem to agree on is that the future is about generating and implementing new ideas and that is what we intend doing in this book.

■ The levels of leadership

One finding that has emerged during the writing of this book is that both change and leadership take place at different levels within the organisation. Although no simplistic two-dimensional model can ever explain and predict fully the nature of such a complex system as a human organisation, used with care, such devices can aid our understanding. We found looking at the operation of an organisation in terms of three levels – strategic, operational and front-line – was a useful way of addressing the issue of change and leadership. Very often, organisations set about creating their own visions and strategies for change through strategic discussions – but with relatively little thought as to how those strategies might be put into practice on a day-to-day basis. Furthermore, even if the operational middle-management levels have had the privilege of being introduced to and even involved in creating the strategies, the impact on the front line is frequently overlooked and often ignored completely.

In contrast, we have found that leaders who are effective at working with change seem to be able to think at these three levels simultaneously and we believe that is a skill which all leaders should develop. One key leadership activity that has emerged is that of 'networking' – building a personal set of contacts across differing functions of the organisation and at differing hierarchical levels. These are the 'integrating leaders' who play a vital role in ensuring that the organisation operates as a cohesive unit rather than as political 'silos', bent on scoring points off each other.

The skill of the effective change leader is to embrace all three levels in the change process. We believe that the key to doing this is to create a strong sense of belonging and emotional alignment to the organisation. As we move onwards into the twenty-first century, there is no doubt that the emotional aspect of business will become more and more significant in determining ultimate success, however that may be measured.

■ Moving forwards

In fact this shift towards the emotional issue is not new. In the early 1980s, Tom Peters with his highly successful book *In Search of Excellence*[8] pointed towards the importance of addressing the 'people issues' as well as business strategy, structure and the other 'hard issues' so common in business literature. Peter Senge in *The Fifth Discipline*[9] advanced our ideas on the learning organisation by promoting both systems thinking in a business sense and the more human aspects of mental models, developing personal mastery, team learning and building shared vision. During the same period, other writers on leadership started to move away from purely behavioural or traits-based models towards thinking about leadership more as an emotionally-based process which affects followers at a deeper, psychological level – the level of inspiration. Warren Bennis and Burt Nanus, for example, pointed towards a 'New Theory of Leadership' in their book *Leaders*[10] which highlighted the differences between management and leadership. Both authors put forward the idea of leaders utilising strategies which have a high emotional impact on the followers: the 'Attention through Vision' is clearly aimed at the inspirational level with communication, the creation of trust and the development of positive self-regard all supporting the emotional dimension.

In more recent times, Bennis has moved from the 'whats' of leadership towards the 'hows' – the mechanisms that leaders at all levels can use effectively to influence their people. This approach has been developed by Jay Conger, a colleague of Bennis. We mentioned Conger earlier in this chapter and he observed twenty-three business leaders operating in a variety of contexts over a twelve-year period. He noted that effective leaders seem to use four vitally important mechanisms in order to influence their people. Firstly, they establish credibility. In the context of change this is vital. It is about the leader being well-informed, handling information appropriately, behaving in a way that inspires confidence and generally winning the confidence of the people. The second point of Conger's approach is that of establishing common ground. People feel threatened in a change situation when they see themselves as potential losers. It is the leader who can see a situation from the other person's viewpoint and then empathise with that individual to establish common aims and objectives who will win the day.

The third idea is that of the use of language. Leaders throughout the ages have known the power of effective oratory and rhetoric. However, in the current business world, much of the emotion seems to have been removed from our language. The effective leader seems to be the individual who can use language effectively to inspire people rather than simply deliver spreadsheets and 'the numbers'.

Finally, Conger points to the emotional aspect of leadership, connecting emotionally with the followers. Once again, we see the implications with regard to moving more towards the importance of Emotional Intelligence rather than intellectual intelligence.

■ The processes created by the leader, not the leader's qualities

It is therefore apparent that leadership is increasingly being recognised as being more than simply the qualities of an individual. It is much more about the processes created by the leader and the impact, largely emotional, on the followers. Coupled with the potential threat and fear aspects of change, we can see just how important it is that effective leaders do master the key principles involved in dealing with people in times of change. The rate of change is accelerating and it is unlikely that we will see it slowing down in the foreseeable future. What we will see, however, is the Drivers of Change making more and more impact on our lives, both at work and in our leisure time.

■ The overview

We have therefore devoted Chapter Two to an exploration of the Drivers of Change because we feel it is vital for any effective change leader to have an overall awareness of the factors which are driving change, both generally and also specifically, related to the individual's own operation.

Chapter Three moves on to consider the nature of leadership in terms of how thought on the subject has developed. Although our own ideas on this aspect of leadership have been presented in a more comprehensive form in our early book *The Business of Leadership*, we feel it is useful to plot the development of thought on leadership because it displays some distinct trends. Firstly, there is a clear shift from the focus on the individual's qualities, through behaviours, towards the idea of effective leaders creating a process whereby they transform the ability of the follower to produce high levels of motivation and performance.

Secondly, the notions of power and authority are clearly moving away from the individual leader towards the generation of energy on the part of the followers. And this leads us to our third clearly identifiable theme, that of the shift from command-and-control-type leadership towards a more empowering style which seeks to unlock the potential in followers, rather than control their behaviour.

The development of our own thoughts on the highly complex topic of leadership also reflects the shift away from the commonly held notion that leadership is 'male, military and Western'. What is now becoming clear is that leadership is a human process which can be and is displayed by both sexes, that all organisations are in need of effective leadership, and that no one part of the world can lay claim to possessing more leadership ability than any other.

In Chapter Four, we consider how organisations are responding to the challenge of change. We see daily examples of downsizing, rightsizing and de-layering and some imaginative reorganisation, together with the subsequent effects on the individuals involved. No longer does anyone realistically believe they will follow a career path during their working life. Promotion is no longer the main driving force in flatter, de-layered businesses. The idea of job enrichment, sideways movements, moving outside the organisation and portfolio lifestyles have become the language of the day. The virtual organisation is becoming a reality for many operations both in the public and the private sector. We are now recognising that it is the development of intellectual capital which is vitally important for the organisation to survive and develop in the future. Luddite reactions to the introduction of technology are no longer tolerated. Every organisation is now having to embrace technology in an unprecedented way. First-line managers have greatly expanded spans of control, middle managers are disappearing and senior management is increasingly realising that it needs to develop its ability at Director and Vice-President level if it is going to retain its leadership credibility.

One unfortunate by-product of the ways organisations are responding is the paradox created by fewer people doing more work and the need for innovation at all levels. Stress in the workplace is increasing dramatically. For example in the United Kingdom, it has been estimated that over 100 million working days are lost each year from a workforce of around 38 million. That translates to between two and three days each year for every person in the workforce. This is a staggering waste of resources.

In addition, stressed people do not produce their best work, particularly in terms of creativity and innovation. For organisations to adapt and embrace change effectively they have to take into account the impact on the people involved. In many respects, workplace stress can be viewed as a result of poor change leadership. Many writers, including Warren Bennis,[11] distinguish between the processes of management and leadership. We would argue that workplace stress is often a by-product of people being over-managed and under-led. Too often management processes fail to take into account the emotional aspects of working. Yet it is those emotional aspects, particularly alignment, which are influenced by effective leadership. Leadership and management are mutually supportive processes. Stress in the workplace is minimised when people feel both well-led and well-managed.

Chapter Five looks in some detail at how human beings respond to change. We explore the notion that people's desire for change and their ability to cope tends, on average, to reduce as they move through life. In contrast to this, the changes to which they have to adapt seem to be escalating on an exponential curve. The impact of this on the individual is considered together with a range of strategic and operational approaches to helping individuals master change for themselves.

Chapter Six is about winning hearts and minds. It is about what the military would call the 'psychological aspects of operations'. Again, we point to the all-important emotional aspects of the human being and how these need to be taken into account by leaders at all levels. Change creates both winners and losers. The winners tend to look after themselves. It is the losers who provide the leader with the greatest challenge. The undermining effects of fear, resistance and negative beliefs provide a major challenge for the effective change leader. We explore how these limiting issues have been addressed in a number of organisational contexts and learn how change can be embraced and developed, rather than feared and opposed. Much of this chapter is based on the outcomes of our interviews with the twenty-five successful 'change leaders' which highlighted five key aspects: creating understanding, communicating the reasons for change, releasing people's potential, setting a personal example and self-pacing.

People who feel involved in the change process tend to react more positively than those who feel change is being forced upon them. We thus look at the issues of delegation, coaching and empowerment in the context of change to see just how possible it is to ensure that people really do 'buy into the change' and become committed. We look at implementing and encouraging change in the middle layers of our de-layered organisation using the important observations of Jon Katzenbach in his book *Real Change Leaders*.[12]

Chapter Seven is about strategy. More accurately it is about creating the conditions for a range of strategies to be effective in creating change, whether the source of the change is from outside the organisation or from within. Fashions change as far as strategy is concerned. Strategic planning was all the rage in the 1970s but seemed to go out of fashion in the more volatile 1980s and 1990s. We believe, however, that unless you have some well-laid-out way of approaching the change situation, your efforts will be doomed. Strategy is important and we believe that every change leader needs to be effective in crafting effective strategies.

Chapter Eight is about evaluating success. Just how does a change leader know if he or she has been effective? We look at various ways of assessing the impact of a change programme from simple attitude surveys to more complex approaches such as scorecards, as well as practical means of measuring both hard and soft issues.

■ Setting the scene

In undertaking our research for this book, we have used a variety of approaches to gaining perceptions from successful change leaders. In particular, one approach we used was a semi-structured interview technique based on the use of a fifteen-point questionnaire which we developed. Many of the leaders we interviewed found this questionnaire both thought-provoking and enlightening. In fact several decided to use it as a management and leadership development tool within their own organisations. We present it as Table 1.2 in this chapter because we feel it may help the reader to focus on the issues of change in their own organisation, and so be more attuned to the subsequent chapters.

Table 1.2 Building a comprehensive picture of Change Leadership

EFFECTIVE CHANGE LEADERSHIP QUESTIONNAIRE

1. What is the most important personal quality which must be displayed by an effective Change Leader?

2. What is the major organisational change in which you have been involved?

3. What helped that change take place effectively?

4. What hindered the implementation of that change?

5. Do you believe that people tend to resist change?

6. What do you believe are the main reasons why people tend to resist change?

7. What is the most important thing to consider when starting a programme to create organisational change?

8. Will leading change tend to be a different process in the future compared to the past?

9. Do you believe that the rate of change is accelerating?

10. What are the main reasons behind your answer to question 9?

11. Is managing and leading change in the present world different from how it has been in the past?

12. How can managers and leaders implement change so that the effects of stress on themselves and others are minimised?

13. How would you go about minimising the effects of negative beliefs on the part of individuals involved in a change programme?

14. Is 'change leadership' different from 'change management'?

15. In your opinion, what is the key to effective change leadership?

■ Summary

This book is an attempt to put right the problems with handling change effectively and it has been a fascinating journey – one which we have been privileged to pursue. We have addressed the key issues of effective change leadership, looking at the drivers of change, the strategies for change, the impact on individuals and also how to evaluate the effectiveness of change leadership.

We have explored some of the work of the world's most perceptive thinkers on the subject of change, and also interviewed many practitioners who are faced with implementing change in an increasingly complex world. What has struck us is the importance of emotion – how people feel about the change process. In order to be more effective at the change process, leaders and managers must be aware of this aspect and also become skilled in its management. Leaders need more than charisma, more than drive and vision, more than intellectual intelligence – even more than emotional intelligence. In order to create the passion for change they need 'Intelligent Leadership'.

The starting point for our journey is to gain an understanding of the Drivers of Change – the subject of our next chapter.

Endnotes

1   Rosabeth Moss Kanter (1988), *The Change Masters*, Unwin
2   Neil Hartley (1996), *Towards a New Definition of Work*, London: RSA
3   The Henley Centre (1998), *2020 Vision*, London: Barclays Life
4   Edgar Schein (1992), *Organisational Culture and Leadership*, Jossey-Bass: San Francisco
5   Daniel Goleman (1996), *Emotional Intelligence*, Bloomsbury
6   Alan Hooper and John Potter (1997), *The Business of Leadership*, Ashgate
7   Jay Conger, 'The Necessary Art of Persuasion', *Harvard Business Review*, July–August 1999
8   Tom Peters and Bob Waterman (1982), *In Search of Excellence*, Harper & Row
9   Peter Senge (1990), *The Fifth Discipline*, Century Business
10   Warren Bennis and Burt Nanus (1985), *Leaders*, Harper & Row
11   Warren Bennis (1989), *On Becoming a Leader*, Arrow
12   Jon Katzenbach, *et al.* (1996) *Real Change Leaders*, Nicholas Brealey

Appetiser

CHAPTER TWO

In this chapter, you will:

■ COME TO REALISE THAT EVEN SUCCESSFUL ORGANISATIONS NEED TO ADAPT TO CHANGES IN THEIR ENVIRONMENT

■ BECOME AWARE OF THE IMPACT OF SOME OF THE POLITICAL, ECONOMIC, SOCIAL AND TECHNOLOGICAL CHANGES WE HAVE SEEN TOWARDS THE END OF THE TWENTIETH CENTURY

■ EXPLORE INTERNALLY AND EXTERNALLY DRIVEN CHANGE

■ BECOME AWARE OF THE FIVE KEY DRIVERS OF CHANGE

■ IDENTIFY THE OPTIMUM SIZE FOR EFFECTIVE CHANGE TEAMS

■ FIND OUT ABOUT THE HALLMARKS OF EXCELLENCE

■ IDENTIFY SOME CORE ORGANISATIONAL VALUES

■ GAIN IDEAS FOR DEVELOPING YOUR OWN CORPORATE VISION TO EXCEED WORLD CLASS PERFORMANCE STANDARDS.

The Drivers of Change

■ The hard reality

It was a cold February day at ABIN Abecor, a prestigious banking institute in Bad Homburg, not far from Frankfurt, Germany. The decision had just been made by the Board of Directors to close the institute after twenty-seven years of providing management education to the European banking industry. Course numbers had grown, the institute attracted leading international speakers in their fields and everything pointed to a successful expansion of the operation in future years. How is it this situation could come about? Certainly it was not an internally driven change. The institute had become a victim of major external change within the European banking industry, which at the end of the 1990s was placing even more of an emphasis on short-term business results at the expense of the longer-term viewpoint.

The Managing Director of ABIN Abecor, Mr Lino Formica, outlined some of the issues that had led to the demise of the institute. Initially, ABIN Abecor had been set up by a number of European Banks joining together to create their own tailormade management development establishment which could prepare managers for both increased multicultural working and to handle change in a fast-moving world. In the three years prior to the decision to shut ABIN, several major European banks had merged and Barclays Bank, the United Kingdom member, had made the decision to withdraw as a member from the institute, and send delegates only when the need arose.

So what, in more detail, were some of the changes that forced ABIN into this unfortunate position? Mr Formica painted an interesting if rather pessimistic picture of banking in Europe at the start of the new millennium. He pointed to increasing competition and a growing need to maintain competitive position by reducing costs as major factors in the changes taking place in the banking world. When an organisation considers cost-cutting, the first area often to be hit is the training and development function. People simply cannot be spared from day-to-day operations to spend time away on training seminars. There is a relentless push to create good short-term financial results at the expense of long-term development.

In the past, the banking world, in common with many public-sector operations, seemed to create the promise of a 'job for life' regardless of the value an individual might or might not add. This comfortable existence has now been swept away in the push for speed of response and gaining the competitive edge. The old paternalistic culture of many organisations has been replaced by a slimmed-down, highly pressurised environment which causes many individuals to burn out prematurely, and which often means that fifty is seen as the age for retirement, albeit on enhanced pension terms.

■ From soft issues to hard issues

In addition to the issue of short-term rather than long-term performance, there seems to have been a shift away from developing the human or 'soft' aspects of 'people skills' towards more technically orientated training. This has meant that institutions such as ABIN, who focused on management development processes for several organisations at the same time, have suffered. It seems that the individual banks are now spending their training budgets on internal training for new products and other technical issues to gain short-term benefits rather than on the cross-cultural, softer issues which ultimately secure the future.

Mr Formica's comments could well be extended to other areas, particularly those such as the defence industries, who seem to have had a comfortable life in the second half of the twentieth century until the end of the Cold War between East and West.

It appears that change is affecting everybody in the business and organisation world. And it is not just external industry changes that cause organisations to review their operations. There are many, many reasons why we are experiencing a greater rate of change than ever before. Technology, politics, social expectations, legislation and a host of other factors are all combining to make the business world extremely volatile. It is almost as if we are on a roller-coaster which is blasting its way around an ever-more-exciting track.

■ An accelerating roller-coaster of change

In particular, in the latter part of the twentieth century we have seen tremendous political change on a scale undreamed of in the past. The collapse of the Berlin Wall, the rise of Eastern Europe, the growth and collapse of Asian economies are just a few examples of how things are changing. One fascinating example is South Africa. In the past decade, South Africa has seen a tremendous upheaval in both its political and social structure and this has impacted greatly on the operation of its business community. In the days of apartheid, the old command and control style of leadership was perhaps more prevalent than in most other areas of the world. Since Nelson Mandela's release from prison and the abolition of apartheid, organisations have had to alter dramatically their policies of employment. It is now a principle that a company should employ a black person in preference to a white if at all possible, even if the qualifications of the white person are superior. This has caused major problems for both operational quality and the development of the intellectual knowledge base of many organisations. However, there are some outstanding examples of forward-looking businesses who have responded to the challenge magnificently.

One is McCarthy Holdings which is the major motor vehicle distributor in South Africa with some 110 new vehicle sales outlets handling some twenty makes of vehicle. Brand Pretorius, the Chief Executive of McCarthy Holdings, has recognised the transition problems and has ensured that the company is heavily involved both in literacy programmes and other ways of promoting a higher level of educational achievement within the country. For example, McCarthy regularly sends four-wheel-drive expeditions into the bush with educational support teams and materials to help in the development of people who would otherwise not experience any real educational process. As the country develops, this effort will bear fruit and is an excellent example of a business taking its social responsibility seriously as well as feeding value back to the community.

■ Change – internally driven or externally imposed?

So change can come from within the organisation or from outside as in the case of ABIN and the South African business community. How does the leader cope with both these situations?

In our previous book *The Business of Leadership*[1] we suggested a number of competencies that leaders need to possess. One of those competencies was 'the leader as change agent' and so we will now explore some of the reasons why this is such an important aspect of leadership.

■ The scales of change

As we have already noted, in basic terms, there are two scales on which change impacts the organisation. Firstly, there are changes that are shaped by factors which range from totally external to those which are internally driven. Secondly, there is a scale of change that has at one end voluntary change and at the other forced change. A key skill in assessing a strategy for change is to position issues according to these two scales that in turn lend themselves to the construction of a matrix on which any specific issue may be mapped (see figure 2.1).

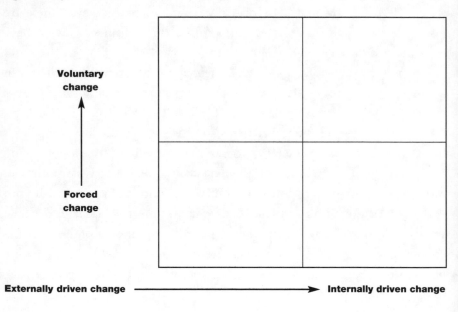

Figure 2.1 The scales of change

In this chapter, we are going to explore the four quadrants suggested by this matrix. As with most models in organisational and human behaviour, the boundaries between the quadrants are not rigid. For example, when a new

CEO is first appointed, she or he may initiate the creation of a new mission statement. Whilst it could be argued that this is primarily a voluntary, internally driven change, the reality is that it is probably the preconceptions and perceptions of the CEO that external factors are forcing the organisation to change. Whether this change is internally or externally driven, voluntary or forced, is thus open to debate.

However, like most models, the matrix does provide a framework to help with the creation of priorities by understanding where the organisation fits into its environment and what steps may be needed to help it adapt to a changing world.

■ The five Key Drivers of organisational change

Although management gurus often agree about very little, one point on which they seem to concur is that we are experiencing an unprecedented speed and rate of change. There are many reasons why this is the case and we will explore some of the factors which are involved. Although these factors initially appear to be primarily external to the organisation, they do have internal consequences.

In basic terms, there are five Key Drivers of Change:

- people
- information
- an increased ability to communicate
- technology
- global competition.

It is difficult to identify a specific time when the world was completely stable. However, over the past three decades it does seem that an identifiable shift has taken place in terms of how we do business. This shift is linked to changes within these five basic areas.

People

There are more people inhabiting our planet than ever before. This means greater demands on resources and we have seen the results of this increasing demand, particularly in the third-world countries. No matter how much external aid is applied, the population explosion simply demands more and more support in terms of food, medical help and so on. Yet, at the same time, the fact that there are more people in the world means that there is the potential for more innovation and creativity than ever before, provided that we tap into the potential abilities that every human being possesses. This leads us to an interesting idea. We have seen the progression of the human race through many stages. First, there was the prehistoric stage where the human race simply came to terms with its environment, living in caves and struggling to survive in a very hostile environment. The next stage was the progression towards the control of the environment and the creation of social structures leading to the rise and the subsequent fall of the early civilisations such as the Greeks and the Romans. As time moved on, we encountered the Agricultural Age, the Industrial Age and so on until we reached, in the 1990s, the Information Age. Where do we go next? What will be the next 'Age' of the human race?

There is a general feeling on the part of many writers that the next age will be focused on tapping into the potential of the human being through the various intelligence factors we possess. Some have even hinted that we will be calling the next age of the human race the 'psycho-zoic age' – the age of human understanding. In the past we have tended to think of intelligence as mainly intellectual. Indeed, most so-called intelligence tests tend to work solely on the basic areas of numeracy and literacy. However, there are many areas in addition to these which add together to create the whole human being. Charles Handy in *The Empty Raincoat*[2] draws our attention to a range of intelligence areas including factual, analytical, linguistic, spatial, musical, practical, physical, intuitive and interpersonal intelligence. Handy admits this list is probably not complete. We can certainly add Emotional Intelligence which according to Daniel Goleman[3] is probably the most relevant for dealing with life's challenges on a daily basis.

However we define intelligence, it is clear that the human being is a complex organism and one which is invariably capable of much more in the way of achievement than is commonly realised. Leaders who are truly effective seem to have the ability to tap into these vast areas of human potential. In the past, we have called them 'transformational' because they transform mediocre activity into excellent activity, and so are inherently part of the change process. However, in recent years, leadership has assumed a higher profile. Rather than being looked at as just part of management, leadership is now seen as complementary to management.

In many books a distinction has been made between 'transactional leadership' and 'transformational leadership'. In the transactional type of leadership process, followers simply obey the orders (implicit or explicit) of their leader and, in doing so, meet certain standards of behaviour because of a contractual arrangement. In transformational leadership, the leader inspires the followers to reach standards of performance which they would not otherwise have reached were it not for the impact of the leader. Thus their behaviour has been 'transformed' by the actions and, perhaps, charisma of the leader. We have come to equate 'transactional leadership' with 'management' and 'transformational leadership' with 'leadership' *per se* in our studies. In essence, we feel that all leadership is inherently transformational if it is leadership rather than management. Thus we would rather talk in terms of 'transcendent leadership' in that effective leaders enable their followers to transcend their current situations and performance levels.

In terms of leadership, this idea of leaders enabling their followers to 'transcend' their current performance levels is a key issue to address. Many organisations in the past looked at people as a cost to be borne rather than an investment to be developed. A key issue for successful change leadership is to develop a culture within the organisation that promotes learning on the part of individuals, teams of individuals and the organisation as a whole. Peter Senge has addressed this issue very comprehensively in his book The Fifth Discipline[4] where he suggests five key factors for creating a learning organisation. These factors include systems thinking, personal mastery, mental models, building shared vision and team learning. All five of these factors could be grouped together under the heading of tapping into the potential of 'people' both individually and in groups. It is interesting to note that Peter Senge and his considerable team of diligent researchers have now turned their attention towards the idea of creating change in organisations to enable those organisations to become Learning Organisations. In their book The Dance of Change[5] they look at a number of ways that the 'learning culture' can be generated within organisations of almost any size – the key to the process, we believe, is unlocking the human potential which always exists within every organisation.

A second way that the 'people' issue is a driver of change concerns human beings in groups rather than as individuals. Traditional ways of looking at change factors in organisational terms focus on both political and social factors. Both of these areas relate to people *en masse* rather than as individuals. And there is an interesting link here with the idea of intelligence. If we take one of the definitions of intelligence as 'appropriate behaviour in a particular situation', then the performance of human beings in terms of intelligence seems to follow an interesting pattern as shown in Figure 2.2. Many writers have observed that teamwork seems to produce more effective working up to a certain number of team members, then that performance tends to become less effective once the team reaches a certain size. We can represent this idea as a graph (see Figure 2.2).

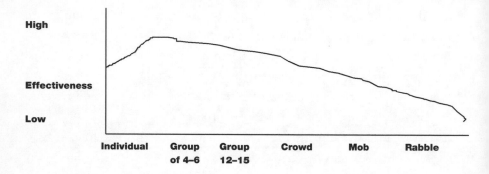

Figure 2.2 The collective performance of people at work

Performance in terms of intelligent action seems to improve when people get together in small groups of four to six. However, once we reach ten or so, then performance levels off and starts to deteriorate until we experience the 'large committee' syndrome and ultimately the often ludicrous behaviour of large crowds and mobs.

What this means for our leader in creating and advancing a change programme is that the key to effective action is to organise your people in small groups. This principle, is of course not new! It is no accident that military, paramilitary and indeed terrorist organisations have used the idea of the 'four-man cell', the 'eight-man section' and so on. Special Forces Units frequently operate in groups of four because experience has shown that it tends to be the most effective way to tap into the potential abilities of the members of the unit. On one level, this idea means that we should organise ourselves for change by working in small teams. The problem with this idea is, however, that these teams can become divisive and cause communication problems. In addition, experience has also suggested that in order to bring about effective change, it is important to create a 'critical mass', a situation where a significantly large proportion of the people involved are committed to the change. We therefore need to bring these small groups together periodically to ensure that the larger team-building effect occurs whilst not developing the less productive side of large group behaviour. One way that this has been achieved by the authors in small, medium and large workshop and seminar groups is to ensure that syndicate and discussion work is undertaken in groups of no more than eight individuals.

Even with a large conference of several hundred it is possible to do this by using a cabaret style of seating with groups of eight people around a table. Where tables involve larger numbers, then these must be subdivided to create a worthwhile environment for the groups to work together effectively.

If we now take a different perspective on people in groups, we can start to think of some of the political changes we have experienced in the last decade of the twentieth century. We have seen the results of the dissolution of the East–West divide. For many, this has created considerable marketing opportunities in the so-called 'Eastern Bloc'. At the same time as the large-scale political divide seems to have dissolved, we have seen ongoing smaller conflict zones such as Bosnia, the Arab–Israeli conflict, and the emergence of despotic leaders such as Gaddafi and Saddam Hussein. These political changes alone have meant that the world has become a very different place with regard to how organisations will operate both now and in the future. We are increasingly seeing companies like Shell coping with international operations, such as their activities in Nigeria which often lead to problems in terms of how they relate to the local government. What these political changes mean is that no longer can we assume the future will be like the past. It seems as though, literally, anything can happen in the world political arena.

And single events can trigger extensive social change within a single country. The death of Diana, Princess of Wales, in August 1997 created a tremendous impression on both the British nation and the world at large. Amongst the outcomes of this very sad situation was that the British Royal Family, who received considerable criticism with regard to how they reacted to Diana's death, had to reassess how they operated. Since August 1997, it has become apparent that the more visible members of the British Royal Family such as the Queen, Prince Charles and Princess Anne are working hard to show the British people that they are in touch with the real world. As an example, the Queen has been photographed by a tabloid newspaper visiting a McDonald's fast food restaurant, and Prince Charles has been working hard to stimulate interest in deprived areas in the United Kingdom such as Cornwall, to help encourage investment in the areas.

Having looked at some of the people issues in political and social terms, we now have to think what this might mean with regard to the leadership of both individuals and groups. Perhaps the most useful term, in respect of change, is expectation. As a result of the political and social changes we have experienced in the recent past, people in general now have higher levels of expectation than ever before. Through the developments in satellite television, people in third-world countries can experience how materialistic societies like Europe and the USA operate. No longer does living in a rural setting in Asia mean that you are cut off from the rest of the world. Baseball games, the Olympics, political dramas and soap operas all play a part in educating the world on the possibilities for lifestyles. In leadership terms, this means that individuals now expect much more of their leaders than ever before. The relevance of the expectation issue to organisational life means that individuals tend to benchmark, often unconsciously, how good organisations operate. And they expect their own leaders to create similar results.

More than ever before, leaders are subject to considerable scrutiny in terms of the results they produce and also with regard to creating an effective organisational climate which meets the expectations of the workforce.

Information

Now let's turn to the information issue. With the creation of the Internet, any individual with access to a computer, a modem and a telephone line now has at her or his fingertips more information than was believed possible only fifty years ago. In April 1999 it was estimated that there were 150 million users worldwide, and that this was increasing by tens of millions per annum. Furthermore, it was anticipated that Internet traffic would exceed telephone traffic by the year 2001.

This has a number of effects. Firstly, there is the problem of information overload. Anyone using an Internet search engine to research a topic soon realises how important it is to specify the topic as accurately as possible. If you simply tap in one key word such as 'leadership' or 'teamwork', it is not unusual to be faced with thousands of occurrences of the word on the Internet. The problem is not the lack of information but finding the information which is useful. This undoubtedly will be a key skill for leaders in the future. It will be vital that leaders at all levels have the ability to sift and sort information to extract the key issues required, and then think with ideas and concepts that are inherently ambiguous and complex.

One area where the explosion in information has been very marked is in the area of electronic or e-mail. It is not uncommon for a typical executive or manager to have a backlog of up to a hundred e-mails, particularly if she or he has been away from the office for a couple of days. Again, the problem is sorting out the important from the trivial. One of the reasons that e-mail seems to have become a challenge for so many people is that it is very easy to create 'cc' lists. By simply calling up a pre-saved list of e-mail addresses, it is possible to send the same message to an unlimited number of people on that list rather than individual messages to each person. Although this can be useful for keeping everybody informed about key issues, it does tend to add to the information overload.

Communication

The learning point for the leader is that of getting the balance right. One of the most common criticisms raised, particularly in organisations, is the communication issue. Almost every organisation we have worked with has had communication on the 'could do better' list. However, it is our feeling that the problem is not that communication does not take place, but rather that individuals feel that they are not always informed about the issues which affect them personally. The balance is hard to achieve but the effective leader does everything to ensure that people do feel they are informed and consulted about the issues that affect them personally.

One of the most significant areas in which management and information are closely linked relates to the role of the middle manager, which has seen tremendous change in the latter part of the twentieth century. Before the use of computers became so widespread, the middle manager was frequently the source of information within the organisation, particularly at the operational level. With the growth of the use of networked computer systems and local personal computers, it seems that the middle manager has become an endangered species – and this has been more apparent with the tendency for organisations to de-layer and flatten their hierarchies.

Very closely linked to the information issue is our increased ability to communicate that information. Within the space of a few years, the communications industry has exploded. Car phones, portable cellphones, pagers, laptop computers, faxes and modems have given us a tremendous ability to communicate almost wherever we are on the planet. And this is leading to unprecedented changes in the nature of work. In certain types of work, it is no longer necessary for individuals to attend their place of work every day. There are now thousands of people worldwide who work effectively from home using personal computers, modems and faxes.

This brings into question the nature of work. What is now becoming even clearer is that people don't simply work in order to gain money to live and to eat. Work provides a socially stimulating environment for many which satisfies social and group needs. Effective leadership of solo workers operating from home must take this into account. The so-called 'virtual organisations' of individuals working at home can provide the leader with a considerable challenge, particularly in the area of creating a team and enabling people to feel part of that team. With virtual organisations, it is vital that the team members do meet on a regular basis to combat the isolation of working alone.

The impact of technology

One of the reasons our ability to communicate has increased so dramatically is the advances in technology that have been made in recent years. Although many of these advances seemed to be pioneered in the space and defence industries, there is almost no part of society worldwide which has not felt the impact of technology. One of the authors was in Bangkok recently and was fascinated to see novice Buddhist monks studying the sayings of Buddha from a CD-ROM on a laptop rather than the established textbooks.

A key trend in technology seems to be that of miniaturisation and micro-miniaturisation. We seem now to be making things smaller and smaller whilst at the same time greatly increasing performance. This is particularly true for the computer industry where computing power seems to double every few months. A state-of-the-art computer bought today is virtually out of date within ninety days. From a leadership viewpoint, there is a resource issue which is raised by this rapid pace of technological change. Should leaders always be at the forefront of technology, with the risk of unreliable equipment which has not been fully developed, or should they wait until industry standards develop and run the risk of being left behind in the race? There is no simple answer to this question. Every industry has its own concerns and it is these issues that ultimately determine the appropriate time to adopt new technological approaches.

Global competition

The fifth of our Key Drivers is ultimately one which is based on the four previous issues. Because we have more people sharing and communicating information using a wide range of modern technology, the world has effectively become a smaller place in terms of perceived markets and perceived competitors. No longer are competitors based in the same geographical region, country or even continent. All businesses have potential competitors from around the world. And organisations are resourcing themselves using the world market as a base. One company in Southern England has its business cards printed in India because they cost substantially less for the same quality as those provided by a local English supplier. In another case, an accountancy practice in the United Kingdom uses a book keeping service in Asia making extensive use of the Internet and e-mail for communication.

One of the main reasons for these examples, which are just two of many, is the apparent differential between the wage rates of the West compared to those of the East. Purchasing managers increasingly ask themselves where they can obtain the required quality of product or service at the cheapest price. Wage rates based on a few pounds an hour rather then tens of pounds per hour make a considerable difference, in fact more than enough to compensate for transportation costs. And this will become even more of a challenge to Western industry as we move more towards knowledge-based industries rather than product-based ones.

■ The shift from West to East

In recent years, the Pacific Rim has gained more and more of a presence in the world marketplace. Despite its financial problems of the late 1990s, there are a number of fundamental forces at play in Asia and the Pacific Rim which mean that the West has to take seriously the so-called 'threat from the East'.

There are a number of interesting trends which we can identify around the Pacific Rim. Firstly, many countries such as Japan and Thailand are shifting from being export-led to being consumer-led. Their internal markets are growing and an increased emphasis seems to be emerging on satisfying those markets. Women are increasingly becoming involved in senior management positions – in excess of 2.8 million Japanese women ran businesses in the late 1990s compared with a fraction of that figure just ten years previously.

In Western countries, including Europe and the USA, we tend to replace people with technology. By contrast, in the East the new technology is embraced whilst at the same time maintaining, or even increasing, the 'head count' in the organisation. You only have to visit the foyer of a leading Asian hotel to see the considerable number of staff ready to help you. In many Western hotels it is often difficult to find one person!

We are conscious that many countries, such as Egypt, have an official policy that no-one can be unemployed. However, we would argue that there is a basic issue here that in the West we have perhaps been misguided in our attempts to create optimum efficiency per employee. By taking this approach, we lose the quality of service that is in line with plenty of staff, ready to serve the customer.

Many Asian companies now focus on expanding networks for their businesses rather than simply developing their own national identity. And partly as a result of this development, intellectual leadership now seems to be shared more throughout the world rather than simply being created in the West. An example of this has been the automobile industry.

In the 1970s it was clear that the Japanese worked hard to imitate the products of the West. Honda, Toyota and Mitsubishi all seemed to be creating replicas of the products of Ford, Leyland and General Motors. However, their imitations were more reliable and in many respects of higher quality than the originals and, as a result, they started to gain more in the way of market share. Eventually, the West woke up to the threat, and we now see many Western car and truck manufacturers actually copying the Eastern product ideas and features. Furthermore, there have been many alliances (such as Rover and Honda), and we have seen a number of Japanese manufacturers, such as Nissan, establish plants in both Europe and the USA.

We are seeing the emergence of the supercities in the East such as Shanghai, Singapore, Hong Kong and Bangkok. No longer is Asia a collection of rural villages, but instead a growing presence of major urban systems, each with high quality hotels and other features to attract both business and visitors.

We see academics becoming entrepreneurs and applying knowledge in a much more vigorous way than appears to be the case in many parts of Europe. We see a shift from copying to creating, and an intense passion and commitment to succeed. Service is something to be proud of in many Asian cultures and this leads to a very positive attitude in terms of service to the customer.

Despite the apparent financial challenges faced by the Pacific Rim, the underlying factors outlined actually predispose the East to become an increasingly important part of global competition and this is a trend to be taken very seriously by the West. As a fundamental external Driver of Change, global competition has been a major force in the marketplace and we will now consider the impact of this and the other four drivers on the Western organisations.

■ How organisations have responded to the five Key Drivers of Change

So what has been the impact of these five Drivers of Change on our organisations?

If we look at a typical large business organisation in the 1970s then there was frequently a hierarchy involved in terms of how the business was organised. The accent was on predictability, rigidity, permanence and certainty. Any change tended to be very measured and to take place in increments rather than in any massive steps. This has now been replaced by insecurity, turbulence and uncertainty because we are becoming increasingly aware that the future will not be like the past. As an example, let us consider IBM, the massive computer company. In the 1970s, IBM was deservedly quoted as a role-model organisation; it was values-driven and one which inspired confidence in both the customer base and the workforce. In fact, a common saying in the 1970s was that 'nobody ever got fired for buying IBM'! Yet in the next decade, it was IBM who failed to identify the massive potential growth in the personal computer market and, as a consequence, in the 1990s, they returned one of the biggest financial losses in corporate history. Lessons have now been learned and IBM is moving onwards to continued success by realising that nobody can rest on their laurels or take anything for granted.

■ From quantity to quality

We have seen the shift from quantity to quality on the part of many producers with a number of businesses now becoming market-led rather than production-led. No longer is it enough to make something and try to sell it. One of the keys to success in business is to find out what the customer wants and needs — and then satisfy those requirements better than the competition. 35

In short, we have seen a shift on the part of successful organisations from a focus on their internal procedures to a greatly increased emphasis on their external relationships, particularly those with the customer, all of whom are now more demanding than in the past, partly because they have a wider choice of suppliers..

■ Organisational excellence as a Driver of Change

We now consider the idea of the organisation focusing on how it can be more effective, particularly in relating to the world around it. During the second part of the twentieth century, a tremendous amount of thought has gone into what we now call 'Organisational Excellence', that is, how effective the organisation is in terms of its operation. Although ultimately the goal of every organisation is to survive and grow, there is an increasing movement towards the idea that it is not just survival that matters. What is really important is being better than the competition over a range of measures. Until the 1980s, those measures were primarily financial, with ratios such as return on investment, growth rates of turnover and profit and so on. As an example of this financial focus, for some twenty-five years the General Electric Company measured its success on seven ratios and twelve trend-lines, virtually all of which were financial in nature.

The seven ratios were:

- profit/sales
- sales/capital employed
- profit/capital employed
- sales/inventories
- sales/debtors
- sales/no. of employees
- sales per £/$ of emoluments.

In addition, the trend-lines monitored were:

- sales in £/$
- orders received
- orders in hand
- net profit

- direct wages
- overhead spend
- capital employed
- stock levels
- trade debtors
- no. of direct and indirect employees
- average wages per hour of direct labour
- export sales.

(Taken from Bob Garratt's perceptive book *The Fish Rots from the Head*).[6]

Since the 1980s, however, other factors seem to be involved in creating an excellent organisation. There has been a definite shift from the so-called hard factors (such as these financial measures) to the softer issues of people, values and satisfaction issues, both for employees and customers. It could be argued that one of the triggers for this shift was the book *In Search of Excellence*[7] by Tom Peters, first published in 1982. Peters said when the book was published that its most notable feature was the set of chapter headings which focused on people and customers rather than financial issues.

If we start to think about internally driven change, it is useful therefore to think about some of the ideas which have been put forward as indicators of organisational excellence. Whilst no simple model serves every business or organisational setting, there are common themes which may be distilled into a useful framework which can then be applied to the real world. So one of the prime sources of internally driven change is that of the organisation itself setting out to become excellent according to a set of prescribed factors. At this stage we will look at some of these factors and then reduce them to form the final framework.

If we think about what characterises a 'healthy' successful organisation, then several factors come to mind. Firstly, such organisations invariably have a sense of purpose, usually articulated through a mission, vision or values statement. The leaders are usually visible within the organisation and the structure matches the strategies in terms of what it is trying to achieve. Employees feel ownership of their particular jobs and decisions are made at the lowest appropriate level.

Motivation levels are usually high, partly because rewards are often linked to achievement. Communication is open and contentious issues are addressed in open forum rather than being 'swept under the carpet' or allowed to degenerate into political arguments. Whilst pursuing the achievement of its vision vigorously, the organisation is grounded in reality and fully aware of the world around it. It manages all its boundaries well including those with its customers, its suppliers and the world at large. We can expand this general perception of the 'healthy organisation' into a more detailed framework which the present authors have had a considerable amount of experience addressing, within a range of organisations. What we have found is that the

Table 2.1 The Hallmarks of Excellence

1. Creating effective Mission, Vision and Values statements.

2. Strategy and integrated planning.

3. Customer issues, both internal and external.

4. How it can develop and learn.

5. How to enable and manage change effectively.

6. How to create continuous improvement at all levels.

7. Adhering to its stated values.

8. Time management and personal focus for everyone in the organisation.

9. Innovative and creative problem-solving at all levels.

10. Effective communications upwards, downwards, sideways and diagonally.

11. Integrating its operation and breaking down barriers between the various departments within the organisation.

12. Developing managers as coaches and enablers rather than as bosses.

13. Identifying and developing competence at all levels.

14. Setting goals and objectives at all levels.

15. Creating the right atmosphere, culture and climate:
    - open communication
    - creating trust
    - producing loyalty

16. Enabling people to enjoy their work.

17. Being aware of the impact of behaviours which show the extent to which it really values people.

18. The power of role models.

19. Revisiting its value set when solving problems.

20. Producing the desire to be the best at what it does at all levels in the workforce.

'successful' organisation pays attention to a number of key issues, as we have shown in Table 2.1.Although this may appear to be a rather daunting list, it is entirely pragmatic and provides a starting point for internally driven organisational change.

Perhaps it is the 'values' issues that are so frequently underestimated. By 'values', we mean the ideas that are felt to be important within the organisation in terms of how it goes about its business. Many fail to grasp the importance of the values issues, particularly the aspect of living the values through behaviour on a day-to-day basis. There have been many examples in our experience of organisations that include in their value statements such lines as 'our people are our most important asset'. If, however, a downturn occurs in business, such companies are often only too ready to make a significant number of employees redundant to save costs in the short term. The true measure of a real value within the organisation is not what it says but what it actually does!

So what are the organisational values that seem to underpin excellent performance? Although there is no single definitive list, the values shown in Table 2.2 frequently appear in one form or another.

Table 2.2 The Values-Driven Organisation

1. We lead by example and act as good role models.

2. We value our external customers and always work in their best interests.

3. We value our workforce and work towards helping them to be as effective as possible.

4. We work towards creating open, effective communication in all directions.

5. We try to promote an atmosphere of honesty, trust and openness by acting with integrity.

6. We encourage people to be successful by recognising their efforts.

7. We are continuously working towards improving the way we do things.

8. We try to build self-esteem on the part of everyone in the organisation.

9. We try to help people to feel good about themselves and in so doing encourage them to give their best performance on a daily basis.

10. We understand the power of rumours and the informal grapevine.

11. We are consistent in our approach to challenging situations in that we live by our values. In short, we walk our talk.

12. We try to create an atmosphere where people enjoy their work.

Although the process of installing some or all of these values is a daunting one, it is important. What, however, is even more important is to ensure that senior management in particular adhere to the stated value set through their actual behaviour, rather than just through their rhetoric.

Table 2.3 In Search of Excellence

IN SEARCH OF EXCELLENCE (TOM PETERS)

1. Action-based

2. Close to the customer

3. Encourages initiative

4. Productive people

5. Governed by values

6. Concentrates on what it does best

7. Simple structure

8. Loose-tight operation

Values underpin organisational excellence. In Table 2.3, the original ideas put forward by Tom Peters in In Search of Excellence are listed. Shortly after Peters' book was published, two British writers Walter Goldsmith and David Clutterbuck[8] carried out some research into what enables British companies to be successful. A somewhat different set of factors emerged and these are shown in Table 2.4.

Table 2.4 The Winning Streak

THE WINNING STREAK (WALTER GOLDSMITH AND DAVID CLUTTERBUCK)

1. Leadership – visibility

2. Autonomy and initiative

3. Control

4. Involvement, communication and developing people

5. Market orientation

6. Focus and doing simple things well

7. Innovation

8. Integrity – customers, employees, suppliers and the public at large

Subsequently, it was interesting to see that a considerable number of the companies cited as examples of excellence by Peters (such as People's Express) ran into difficulty during the 1980s, despite having displayed some or all of the characteristics of excellence. Peters has a very plausible explanation for this situation. When the original research for the book was carried out during the 1970s, the world was a more stable environment with more predictable cost trend-lines and market forecasts. During the 1980s, the world became unstable, both politically and commercially, and the original model of excellence put forward by Peters did not address the issue of change. In his later book Thriving on Chaos[9] a much simpler approach to management excellence was put forward that enhanced the ability of the organisation to deal effectively with change. Table 2.5 shows the five factors which Peters suggested would underpin the prescription for a management revolution. In many respects, this has proved to be one of the most useful 'change focus' models – and it seems to have had a considerable impact on managers worldwide.

Table 2.5 Thriving on Chaos

THRIVING ON CHAOS (TOM PETERS)

1. Customers

2. Innovation

3. Empowering people

4. Appropriate leadership at all levels

5. Systems that work

Effective change leadership driven from the inside is not just the province of the organisational development experts. The Total Quality Movement, and the subsequent approaches of continuous performance improvement, have provided us with a useful systems approach to business excellence. Figure 2.3 is based on the model produced by the British Quality Foundation and is important as it shows effective leadership as a prime driver for organisational excellence. We have taken the liberty of modifying some of the labels in the boxes to reflect our suggestion that quality is not just about 'system', but the synergistic mixture of 'passion plus system'!

We can see that even in the statistically orientated world of total quality

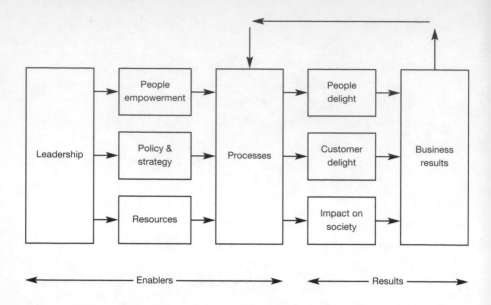

Figure 2.3 A development of the business excellence model

that organisational excellence is driven by effective leadership which includes setting a vision, creating a sense of purpose including a mission statement, identifying and working according to an agreed set of values, and actually behaving in a way that shows adherence to those values.

So with all these attempts at defining a framework for change which triggers internally driven change, where are we? It does seem that the various models of organisational excellence have considerable overlap with regard to the areas they address. We have therefore proposed a composite model which we will call the 'World Class Profile', which suggests ten key areas that organisations must address if they are to respond effectively to the five external Drivers of Change of people, information, communication, technology and global competition. Table 2.6 shows the World Class Profile in questionnaire form which can be used to gain a common perception within a management team of:

1.   how good the organisation is, in current terms, on each of the dimensions; and
2.   whether it is improving on those dimensions.

The World Class Profile addresses five key business issues and five human

Table 2.6 The World Class Profile

THE WORLD CLASS BUSINESS PAYS ATTENTION TO THE FOLLOWING BUSINESS AND PEOPLE ISSUES:

Thinking about your organisation, rate it with marks out of 10 for each of the following aspects . . .	This time last year	Today
1. Leadership, direction and focus	——	——
2. Sound organisation and financial competence	——	——
3. Customer orientation and communication	——	——
4. It is sensitive to its environment	——	——
5. It anticipates change, embraces change and innovates	——	——
6. Values, respects and develops its people	——	——
7. Breeds positive beliefs and attitudes	——	——
8. Builds teams that learn together	——	——
9. Encourages systems thinking and likes people to think 'outside the box'	——	——
10. Becomes a good place to be	——	——
	LAST YEAR	NOW
TOTAL SCORES / 100	☐	☐

issues. It must be stressed that the profile is essentially a 'big picture' framework. Each item is capable of considerable subdivision and expansion, according to the needs of the particular organisation.

Leadership and management are both addressed in the first two dimensions and item 3 assesses the extent to which the organisation focuses on its customers. Item 3 does not necessarily just refer to the external customer but may include internal customer aspects as well. The relationships between departments within the same organisation are often worse than between the organisation and its competitors. It is therefore vital to ensure that departments co-operate effectively on a daily basis.

Item 4 is about sensitivity to the total environment in which the **43** organisation finds itself. This is not just the market environment but includes the five Key Drivers already discussed. In particular, the social, political and technological drivers must be continually monitored to ensure that the organisation maintains and develops its position and this leads naturally to item 5 which is about effective change management.

The people issues are addressed in items 6 through 10. In particular, the notion of valuing, respecting and developing its people is a key area. In the United Kingdom, there has been a real effort made in this area through the Investors in People Programme which sets out standards of performance for developing the workforce. There is more to this issue than at first might be realised. We are moving towards a world where knowledge and intellectual capital are probably the most important assets possessed by an organisation. Rather than see people as a cost to be minimised, the emphasis is now increasingly upon the human resource being looked at as an asset to be developed. Table 2.7 outlines the areas that are identified in the National Standards for Investors in People.

Table 2.7 The UK Investors in People Approach

STANDARDS FOR THE UK INVESTORS IN PEOPLE AWARD

These revolve around a number of key issues:

1.1　The commitment from top management to train and develop employees is communicated throughout the organisation.

1.2　Employees at all levels are aware of the broad aims or vision of the organisation.

1.3　The organisation has considered what employees at all levels will contribute to the success of the organisation and has communicated this to them.

1.4　Where representative structures exist, communication takes place between management and representatives on the vision of where the organisation is going and the contribution that employees (and their representatives) will make to its success.

2.1　A written but flexible plan sets out the organisation's goals and targets.

2.2　A written plan identifies the organisation's training and development needs, and specifies what actions will be taken to meet these needs.

2.3　Training and development needs are regularly reviewed against goals and targets at the organisation, team and individual levels.

2.4　A written plan identifies the resources that will be used to meet training and development needs.

2.5　Responsibility for training and developing employees is clearly identified and understood throughout the organisation starting at the top.

2.6   Objectives are set for training and development actions at the organisation, team and individual levels.

2.7   Where appropriate, training and development objectives are linked to external standards, such as National Vocational Qualifications (NVQs) or Scottish Vocational Qualifications (SVQs) and units.

3.1   All new employees are introduced effectively to the organisation and all employees new to a job are given the training and development they need to do the job.

3.2   Managers are effective in carrying out their responsibilities for training and developing employees.

3.3   Managers are actively involved in supporting employees to meet their training and development needs.

3.4   All employees are made aware of the training and development opportunities open to them.

3.5   All employees are encouraged to help identify and meet their job-related training and development needs.

3.6   Action takes place to meet the training and development needs of individuals, teams and the organisation.

4.1   The organisation evaluates the impact of training and development actions on knowledge, skills and attitude.

4.2   The organisation evaluates the impact of training and development actions on performance.

4.3   The organisation evaluates the contribution of training and development to the achievement of its goals and targets.

4.4   Top management understands the broad cost and benefits of training and developing employees.

4.5   Action takes place to implement improvements to training and development identified as a result of evaluation.

4.6   Top management's continuing commitment to training and developing employees is demonstrated to all employees.

Tables 2.6 and 2.7 provide a useful reference for top management to identify the extent to which it really does believe in developing the employees.

Creating an environment where people have positive beliefs and attitudes about their work is important and this is included as item 7 in Table 2.6. The Total Quality Movement started off as being primarily concerned with quality systems and such tools as statistical process control. However, it has been shown time and time again that Total Quality Programmes have a high rate of failure, as high as 85%, unless the human issue is addressed correctly.

Quality, as Tom Peters says, is about system plus passion. It is the creation of passion which is the real challenge, and passion results from positive beliefs which show themselves as positive attitudes to working for quality, and also producing excellent results in all the areas of organisational life.

The importance and power of effective teamwork has already been mentioned. Teams that operate well together tend to cope with pressure and produce excellent results compared with isolated activity and dysfunctional groups. So often the teamwork issue is restricted to front-line operation such as service teams, production teams and shop floor activity such as manu- facturing cells. The reality is, of course, the teamwork becomes even more important as you move up the hierarchy of the organisation. Jon Katzenbach in his article 'The Myth of the Management Team'[10] has pointed this out most convincingly. It is a sad fact of most businesses that the higher you go in the organisation, the less the teamwork and the greater the incidence of political turf guarding. Boards of Directors, Presidents and Vice-Presidents need the skills of effective teamwork even more than the front-line employees if the organisation is to function effectively.

Item 9 on the World Class Profile is about corporate creativity. Most people tend to be overfocused on their own particular part of the organisation. Peter Senge has pointed this out most graphically in *The Fifth Discipline* with his concept of the Beer Game. In short, this exercise is a fictitious case study of a particular brand of beer for which a sudden market demand arises due to the beer appearing in a pop video. Various individuals play the roles of the retailers, wholesalers, distributors and brewery who all fail to anticipate the demand for the beer. Within quite a short space of time, the players all descend into panic moves to defend their own positions and a crisis results where initially there is a failure to supply the market. Ultimately, the systems ends up overproducing when the market demand has subsided and everybody blames everybody else for the subsequent shambles. Although there are many learning points of the Beer Game, one of the prime ones is that we all need to look at the wider picture before making a change to take into account how it will affect our colleagues. The expression 'thinking outside the box' relates to the idea that, so often, it is as if we are each trapped inside a specific organisational box, unable to see situations from the viewpoints of others.

Finally, the tenth item is inherently impossible to define scientifically. The notion of work becoming 'a good place to be' is contrary to many people's concept of the nature of work. For many, work is a black cloud to be entered on Monday morning, endured for five days and then to be escaped from as soon as possible on Friday afternoon. This is hardly the way to create organisational excellence. We need to create workplaces where people enjoy their work and where they look forward to being part of it on a daily basis. Although this aspect of work has not received much attention in the past, it is perhaps THE most important workplace issue we need to address, particularly in view of the much publicised figures relating to the cost of stress in the workplace.

So far, we have looked at the drivers of organisational change from the viewpoint of externally driven change, and those drivers which result from the leader's perception of internal changes that need to take place to enable the organisation to adapt to its surroundings. It is interesting at this stage to identify some aspects of change and the leadership issues involved.

Firstly, what works in one organisation at one time won't necessarily work in another place at another time. There are no hard and fast rules about what will or will not work. The leadership skill is to identify the most promising areas, initiate some changes, observe the results and then modify the change programme if appropriate. Secondly, we are no longer a 'fat economy'. We no longer have excess cash and are forced to set priorities. Thirdly, in influencing others to accept change, promotion is no longer so readily available as a reward system. Leaders need to be able to persuade people to follow with rewards other than purely financial.

There do seem to be some significant dilemmas which leaders face when dealing with the Drivers of Change.

Firstly, there is the need for experimentation *versus* a need to be right. So often in taking risks in developing a change programme, we come across what has been called Murphy's Law – if a thing can go wrong, it will go wrong! So often it seems that it's the thing you decide to ignore which turns out to be the most important factor. Table 2.8 reminds us in a light-hearted way of some of the human obstacles to creating change!

Identifying exactly when to start is a key skill. There is often a clash between the idea of powerful leadership *versus* empowered followers. To what extent should the leader give detailed direction? To what extent should he or she seek alignment on the part of the employees on a voluntary basis rather than through force?

It is important to keep managing the present whilst also managing the change – and the appropriate mix of time spent on these two areas is vital.

Handling the environment whilst, at the same time, building the internal

Table 2.8 Human obstacles to creating change

There are always many reasons for not changing yet:

- 'it isn't the right time'

- 'we don't have the right resources'

- 'it'll be better next year'

- 'we need more data'

- 'we need a committee to look into it'

organisation and also creating a market-led organisation which is internally healthy, is a key issue to be addressed.

Finally, the whole area of beliefs is important. To what extent can simple beliefs be applied to complex issues? What is more important, details or the wider viewpoint?

In creating the change, are there values which clash?

There is no doubt that a sound awareness of the Drivers of Change both internal and external, together with appropriate decision-making in terms of voluntary and forced change, is vital to an effective leadership process.

Perhaps the key to effective leadership for the future will be along the lines of the 'Persuasive Leadership' model suggested by Jay Conger which we have already mentioned. Conger, in studying some twenty-three highly successful executive business leaders over a twelve-year period, found that they all displayed four characteristics in common. Firstly, they were believable, operating from a sound knowledge base and giving reasons for any changes in operating approach. Secondly, they looked for the common ground, for areas of mutual agreement with the individuals they were attempting to influence. This is vital if we want to overcome the negative beliefs so often encountered in major change programmes. A third area was about the effective presentation of evidence and the use of language. This points, once again, to the importance of the leader as communicator. Finally we have the idea of the leader having a good understanding of the emotional frame in which any change is taking place. Once again, the issue of Emotional Intelligence becomes relevant. Human beings are emotional creatures and effective change leaders must take this into account.

■ Summary

So to summarise, what can we deduce from our consideration of the Drivers of Change? Firstly, change can be voluntary or forced or a combination of both drivers and either internally or externally driven. It is convenient to show this as a four-part matrix, each element of which has its own particular challenges. Whatever the nature of the challenge, the key to creating a passion for change throughout the organisation is through intelligent leadership and the effective application of the principles of Emotional Intelligence. Leadership is no longer about command and control and forcing people to conform. It is about winning hearts and minds through effective persuasive leadership using relationship and rapport skills, and also seeing the situation from other people's viewpoints. The five major change clusters of people, information, communication, technology and global competition are here to stay. These are the Key Drivers of Change and they are what the intelligent leader has to come to terms with and use to his or her advantage.

If, as leaders, we create a compelling vision of the future that is value-driven and which takes into account the World Class Factors, then we can harness the power of the Drivers of Change rather than fight against them.

Dealing with the Key Drivers of Change and the associated human responses is a matter of persuasion and Jay Conger has given us a useful signpost in his four-part approach of gaining credibility, establishing the common ground, presenting evidence and gaining a sound understanding of the emotional framework in which a change programme is taking place.

Endnotes

1   Alan Hooper and John Potter (1997), *The Business of Leadership*, Ashgate
2   Charles Handy (1994), *The Empty Raincoat*, Hutchinson
3   Daniel Goleman (1996), *Emotional Intelligence*, Bloomsbury
4   Peter Senge (1990), *The Fifth Discipline*, Century Business
5   Peter Senge (1999), *The Dance of Change*, Nicholas Brealey
6   Bob Garratt (1996), *The Fish Rots from the Head*, HarperCollins
7   Tom Peters (1987), *In Search of Excellence*, Harper & Row
8   Walter Goldsmith & David Clutterbuck (1984), *The Winning Streak*, Penguin
9   Tom Peters (1987), *Thriving on Chaos*, Pan Books
10   Jon Katzenbach et al. 'The Myth of the Management Team', *Harvard Business Review*, November–December 1997

Appetiser

CHAPTER THREE

In this chapter, you will:

■ FIND OUT MORE ABOUT CURRENT THOUGHT ON WHAT LEADERSHIP IS ALL ABOUT

■ COME TO REALISE THAT LEADERSHIP IS NOT JUST MALE, MILITARY AND WESTERN

■ GAIN AN AWARENESS OF HOW THOUGHT ON LEADERSHIP HAS DEVELOPED DURING THE TWENTIETH CENTURY

■ UNDERSTAND THE DIFFERENCE BETWEEN TRANSACTIONAL AND TRANSFORMATIONAL LEADERSHIP AND HOW THIS HAS LED TO THE NOTION OF 'TRANSCENDENT' LEADERSHIP

■ IDENTIFY THE DIFFERENCES BETWEEN LEADERSHIP AND MANAGEMENT

■ IDENTIFY THE LEADERSHIP DILEMMAS OF CONSTANT CHANGE

■ FIND OUT ABOUT THE SEVEN KEY LEADERSHIP COMPETENCIES

■ IDENTIFY THE ROLE OF THE LEADER IN DEVELOPING INTELLECTUAL CAPITAL IN THEIR ORGANISATION.

The Essence of Leadership

■ What is leadership?

Leadership is such a fascinating subject. It is a word that is used almost daily by people, either in reference to their experience at work or their reactions to the example set by political, business, community and sporting leaders. It is also a word that appears daily in newspapers, on television and on radio. But do we know what we mean when we use the word 'leader'? What lies at the core of this word? And how does this relate to the constantly changing world that is now our environment?

This chapter explores the essence of leadership by, initially, looking at how the thinking on this topic has developed over the last fifty years, and then by considering the competencies of leadership. It concludes with an examination of the leadership dilemmas of managing constant change. This will enable us to relate the thinking to the practicalities of the issues which are faced every day by leaders operating at all levels.

■ The development of leadership thought

Until the Second World War of 1939–45, leadership was largely a mystical subject linked closely to class issues and social position. The study of leadership as a subject really developed in the 1940s in the wake of the Second World War, probably due to the demonstration of leadership by individuals coping with enormous responsibilities amidst the chaos of that worldwide conflict.

It is also significant that the instigator of the war, Adolf Hitler, held the title of Der Führer – the leader.

Academics were able to draw on rich material for their research amongst the military and political leaders of that era. It is therefore hardly surprising that the first theory to emerge was that of the 'Great Man' or the 'Qualities' approach – and we are not being politically incorrect by calling such theories 'Great Man' rather than 'Great Person'. For many people, up until the latter part of the twentieth century, as we have already mentioned, leadership has been thought of as a concept which is primarily male, military and Western. This, of course, is far from the truth. History has shown us female leaders of outstanding ability such as Indira Gandhi, Golda Meir, Margaret Thatcher and Benazir Bhutto.

All organisations through history have needed and displayed varying levels of success with their own leadership. And the world does not just consist of Europe and America! Leadership was, is and always will be a global issue and one which involves all people, whatever their organisational or social setting. However, it has to be acknowledged that the military world has created a number of significant leaders. Many of these leaders and their contributions to the human experience have been discussed by John Adair in his excellent book *Great Leaders*.[1] However, whilst it is tempting to focus on the successful military leaders in history, it is important to realise that whenever human strengths are involved, if those strengths are carried to excess, they can become weaknesses.

This is pointed out most convincingly by Norman Dixon in his book with the irreverent title *On the Psychology of Military Incompetence*.[2] Dixon argues that the very traits often much admired by the military in times of crisis can lead to poor decision-making. He proposes the idea that individuals attracted to strongly hierarchical organisations, where power is very obviously displayed through the use of uniforms with badges of rank and so forth, are prone to a psychological condition known as 'cognitive dissonance'. This was first proposed by psychologist Leon Festinger in 1957,[3] who suggested that individuals with a strong need for structure and whose thinking was decisive in 'black and white' terms, have a tendency to make decisions too quickly, on less than adequate data. Now it can be argued that the only reason a decision needs to be made is when the data is lacking to such an extent that the correct decision to make is not obvious. However, Festinger's point is that individuals who tend to suffer from cognitive dissonance have a problem dealing with new information after they have made their decision, when that new information suggests they have made the wrong choice.

More balanced individuals will probably alter their viewpoint in the light of the new information and may even make a subsequently different choice.

The person experiencing cognitive dissonance will not find it easy to do this. In fact their response tends to be to reinforce the first decision to an extent that their behaviour becomes almost bizarre. It is as if they are experiencing a deep unconscious conflict between two beliefs. One belief is that it is important that they make a decision quickly and stick to it – if they change their decision they will be seen to be weak, vacillating and lacking in leadership. At the same time, however, they are experiencing a growing realisation that the situation is not as they had first thought, that their initial judgement may have been flawed and that they should alter their decision to respond to the new information. Dixon cites many examples of how this apparent internal conflict experienced by well-known historical military figures has led to catastrophic consequences in battle.

So despite their preoccupation with the subject of leadership, the military community has not always been as successful at its application as they would like to think.

Furthermore, the problem with the 'Great Man' Approach was that it led to an impasse when trying to identify how to develop effective leaders, since it was almost impossible to produce a definitive list of leadership qualities. Despite this obvious flaw, this theory still has its followers today, many of whom believe that leaders are 'born' – not 'made'.

It was the poorly defined aspects of the Qualities Approach which led thinkers to develop the Situational Approach (see Figure 3.1). This centred on the idea that it was knowledge and appropriateness to the situation which defined the most effective leader. The problem with this theory was that it was too rigid, because it implied that one individual would be appropriate for one situation, but not for another. In reality, leaders are required to be sufficiently flexible to cope in a number of different scenarios.

It was this frustration with both these two approaches that led researchers in the 1960s to reconsider their thoughts on leadership. In the United States, a number of research projects were undertaken to examine the behavioural aspects. Interestingly, these were largely funded by the military. The research into the behaviour patterns of leaders was carried out by Ohio State and Michigan universities, exemplified by the work of Ralph Stogdill (1974).[4] The culmination of all this research led to the focus on two factors: the 'concern for people' and 'concern for the task', which is the basis of the task–relationship idea of leader behaviour.

The realisation of this aspect of behaviour naturally led research into 'Contingency' Theory which concentrated on the context of the leadership

LEADERSHIP — A COMPOSITE APPROACH

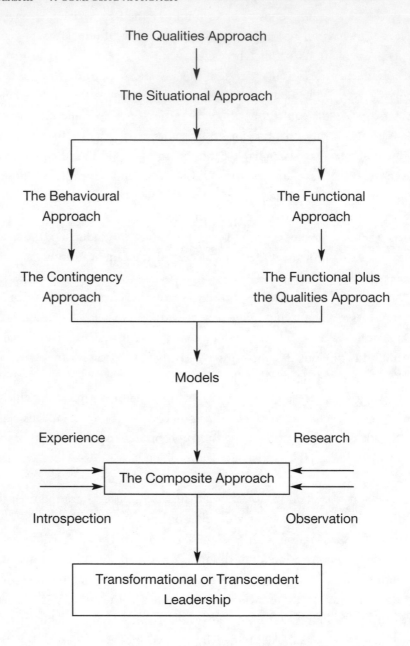

The Qualities Approach

The Situational Approach

The Behavioural
Approach

The Functional
Approach

The Contingency
Approach

The Functional plus
the Qualities Approach

Models

Experience

Research

The Composite Approach

Introspection

Observation

Transformational or Transcendent
Leadership

Figure 3.1 An overview of the development of thought on leadership

activity. In particular, it focused on the ability of the leader to handle that context. This was the focus of research in the 1970s, and featured the work of Fiedler (1969).[5] Hersey and Blanchard (1988)[6] took a slightly different approach in their Situational Life Cycle Theory in that they looked at the appropriate mix of task and relationship behaviours operating in the leadership situation. They suggested that there is an optimum mix which depends on the level of maturity of the team of followers. Immature groups which have not worked together need much more direction than those groups which have become teams, in the true sense of the word, and who are both motivated and competent to work with minimal direction.

Whilst this behaviourally based work was going on in the USA, John Adair (during his time as a military historian at the Royal Military Academy, Sandhurst in the UK) developed an interest into the factors which led to effective leaders gaining the support of followers. His interest had been aroused by observation of officer cadets at Sandhurst and it led him to the idea that leaders should take care of three needs: those of the task; those of the team; and those of the individual (see Figure 3.2). This work in the UK (known as The Three Circles) has proved a remarkably robust model. It formed an important part of the Functional Approach.

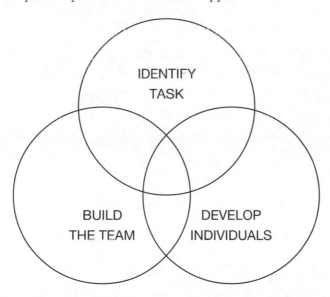

Figure 3.2 John Adair's Three Circle Approach to leadership functions

Adair's work was particularly important in two aspects: first, it led thinking towards the idea of leadership development; and second, it split the 'people' aspect into two parts – the team and the individual.

Leadership and change – the Composite Approach

The evolution of leadership thought has gathered momentum in the last twenty years and a number of writers have explored the relationship between leadership and change. This research has traced the practical development in organisations as they have experienced the change process, and it has also involved the researchers proposing models to assist with that change. This has resulted in a dynamic relationship between the writers and the practitioners, which is still continuing. We have called this period the 'Composite' Approach. The key to the Composite Approach is the recognition that effective leadership is not learned from a book by studying and adhering to one particular leadership model.

Whilst an awareness of a range of leadership models can be useful in short-circuiting the negative side of experience, it is the mix of observation, experience, exposure to effective role models, research and introspection which underpin truly effective leadership development. Leadership has to be a transformational process, or as we call it a transcendent process, unlocking the potential contained in every human being, rather than being a contractual or transactional arrangement where people perform simply to gain personal rewards, financial or otherwise.

There have been a number of people who have contributed to the thinking of leadership thought and development in the 1980s and 1990s. The American contribution has included authors such as Bernard Bass (1990) with his exploration of 'Transformational Leadership'; Warren Bennis (1989) with his insight into the ingredients that combine to make an effective leader; and John Kotter's (1990) examination of the difference between leadership and management in meeting the challenge of change. Other American thinkers include Rosabeth Moss Kanter (1983, 1989) who is a leading authority on the management of change; Tom Peters and Robert Waterman (1982, 1987) with their focus on excellence and managing chaotic change; Peter Senge's (1990) exploration of the 'learning organisation'; and Jon Katzenbach's (1993, 1996, 1998) examination of effective teamwork.

The British contribution has been led by John Adair who pioneered the thinking in UK in the early 1980s through his work on 'action-centred leadership' (1983) and then developed it further by looking at examples of the great leaders throughout history (1989), and by exploring the practical aspects of leadership (1998). Over the same timescale Meredith Belbin, a contemporary of Adair, has developed his thinking about the various roles that make up a team (1993) and the shape of organisations (1996). Another contemporary, Charles Handy, has made an invaluable contribution to this whole area through his lifetime study into the future of work and organisations (1985, 1990, 1994). Bob Garratt has paralleled Peter Senge's work by exploring the learning organisation (1994), whilst Philip Sadler has provided a comprehensive overview of leadership (1997). Our own input (1997) to this debate has focused on the competencies of leadership and on the concept of the 'learning leader'.

The interesting aspect of the matching work on the USA and UK has been the mutual respect that authors from both sides of the Atlantic have for each other. For instance, Adair and Bennis often share a platform together, and they are both Visiting Professors at Exeter University's Centre for Leadership Studies; and Bennis and Handy have a long friendship going back to the days when the latter was a mature MBA student at MIT's Sloan School of Management, where Bennis was on the Faculty.

■ From management to leadership

This period has also seen the emphasis shift from management to leadership, fundamentally brought about by the requirement for people to cope with the management of change. As we have seen above, John Kotter's work has included a detailed study of the different aspects of management and leadership. Table 3.1 is based on his work and considers these as two separate processes, in tabulated form, against certain criteria. The suggestion is that management is about planning, organising and controlling which implies handling financial and material resources, as well as people. On the other hand, leadership is about setting direction, aligning people – and motivating and inspiring them. It is purely about people.

This thinking is extended further in Table 3.2, which is based on Warren Bennis' work. This considers differences between the behaviours and the actions of a leader and a manager. It will be seen that the list on the left is

Table 3.1 Management and leadership as two separate processes

(Based on an idea of John Kotter in A Force for Change, The Free Press, 1990)

	Management	Leadership
What are we setting out to do?	Planning and Budgeting – establishing detailed steps and timetables for achieving needed results, and then allocating the resources necessary to make that happen.	Establishing direction – developing a vision of the future, often the distant future, and strategies for producing the changes to achieve that vision.
How do we encourage our people to deliver the required results?	Organising and staffing – establishing some structure for accomplishing plan requirements, staffing that with individuals, delegating responsibility and authority for carrying out the plan, providing the policies and procedures to help guide people or systems to monitor implementation.	Aligning people – communicating the direction by words and deeds to all those whose co-operation may be needed so as to influence the creation of teams and coalitions that understand the vision and strategies and accept their validity.
Making it happen	Controlling and problem-solving – monitoring results against plan in some detail, identifying deviations and then planning and organising to solve these problems.	Motivating and inspiring – energising people to overcome major political, bureaucratic and resource barriers to change by satisfying very basic, but unfulfilled, human needs.
Outcomes	Produces a degree of predictability and order, and has the potential of consistently producing key results expected by stakeholders (e.g., being on budget, etc.)	Produces change, often to a dramatic degree, and has the potential of producing extremely useful change (e.g., new products that customers want, new approaches to staff relations that help the organisation to develop).

about management control, predictability and short-term results. In contrast, the right-hand list is more emotional; it is about unlocking human potential and working towards a more visionary future. The short-term approach of the industrial nations of the Western world, particularly in the last two decades, indicates that the emphasis has been on the left-hand column rather than a balanced mix of both approaches. The balance now needs to be redressed by developing the leadership ability of all managers at every level within the organisation.

Having said that, we are not suggesting that an individual should become either a leader or a manager. For organisations to be successful in today's environment of constant change it is necessary to have some people who are good at both. Whilst many organisations are well-administered and well-controlled, few have the appropriate vision, innovation and original thinking.

Table 3.2 The Manager and the Leader

(With acknowledgement to Warren Bennis from his book On Becoming a Leader*)*

The Manager	The Leader
Administers	Innovates
Is a copy	Is an original
Maintains	Develops
Focuses on systems	Focuses on people
Relies on control	Inspires trust
Short-range view	Long-range view
Asks how and when	Asks what and why
Eye on the bottom line	Eye on the horizon
Imitates	Originates
Accepts the *status quo*	Challenges the *status quo*
Obeys orders without question	Obeys when appropriate but thinks
Does things right	Does the right things
Is trained	Learns
Managers operate within the culture	*Leaders create the culture*

■ From Transactional and Transformational Leadership to Transcendent Leadership

The movement from Transactional to Transformational Leadership occurred both in the academic discourse, which started with James McGregor Burns' 1978 book *Leadership*, and in the changing style of the practical leadership of organisations; a move from 'command and control' to 'empowerment. Philip Sadler[7] draws a neat distinction between the two: 'Transactional Leadership occurs when managers take the initiative in offering some form of need satisfaction in return for something valued by employees, such as pay – Transformational Leadership, however, is the process of engaging the commitment of employees in the context of shared values and shared vision.'

The position today is that the Composite Approach has led to Transformational Leadership as organisations experience unprecedented change, and the close relationship between thinkers and practitioners continues to develop. We have already argued in Chapter Two that 'Transformational Leadership' is in effect true 'leadership', so we prefer to use the title 'Transcendent Leadership' to describe this process of the leader engaging the emotional support of the followers. Indeed, many of the most forward-thinking of the academics spend a significant part of their time as consultants, both trying to help organisations cope with change – and also trying to understand the fundamentals of the problems. Nobody has all the answers – everybody is at the cutting-edge.

The realisation that the key requirement today is to enable people to be 'transformed' or to 'transcend' has arisen from the practical implications of the speed of change. As we have seen from Chapter Two, amongst the Drivers for Change have been technology and communications. Another key factor has been the recession in the early 1990s, which forced organisations to take decisions that they might otherwise have avoided. It also made them realise that people really were their most important asset. Furthermore, if the management did not recognise this fact, both in the way they rewarded their workforce and in their own behaviour, the more talented sought employment elsewhere. The conditions for such movement were made easier by the development of a portfolio lifestyle which was a by-product of the recession. A 'portfolio' approach acknowledges that there is more to life than just work. Whilst it is necessary to work in order to earn sufficient money to meet one's needs, activities done purely for interest (such as doing charity work or sitting on a school board) allow for a more balanced life.

Another consequence of the recession has been the downsizing of organisations, which has impacted, in particular, on the young men and women leaving the colleges and universities in the mid-1990s. They were told that there were no more 'jobs for life', and that most of them could expect to do five different jobs in their lifetime. As so often in the past, this new lifestyle was pioneered in the USA and, increasingly, it has become a model in the UK.

■ From solo leadership to team leadership

All of this development has impacted on the style of leadership and it has been fundamental in the evolution of Transcendent Leadership. This has included a movement from solo to team leadership; a requirement for remote leadership; an increasing need to lead *ad hoc* teams; and the realisation that 'e-mail' leadership is becoming a growing necessity. As organisations have delayered and become flatter, so leaders have empowered their people more. This has resulted in a voluntary decision by many of them to allow their power to be eroded, and also to share more information. Senior managers have not been given sufficient credit for this shift in their behaviour, which has been all the more remarkable because it has been voluntary. However, such has been the force of change that there has been little option if they wanted to ensure that their organisations continued to be effective in an environment of continual change.

Perhaps the most remarkable aspect of this transformation has been its speed. In the dying years of the twentieth century, leaders who behaved as they used to at the end of the 1980s have appeared anachronistic, old-fashioned and out of touch. Within ten years the style of leadership has changed fundamentally.

Or has it? Although the formalisation of the 'approach' has become recognised as transformational (as opposed to contingency or situational), the fundamentals of leadership have always been the same, embracing vision, inspiration, example and achieving results. In the past this was exemplified by such leaders as Viscount Slim and Sir Ernest Shackleton. It is only the context and the speed of change that are different. What is now recognised is that in order to transform their people, managers need to be competent leaders. Furthermore, effective leaders do certain things that ineffective leaders do not. This has led to the identification of certain leadership competencies.

■ The leadership competencies

First, leaders need to set the direction for the organisation, which incorporates a vision of the future. Second, effective leaders are influential examples and role models because they are aware of the fact that people are more influenced by what they see than by what they are told. Third, they are effective communicators, both in communicating the vision, and also inspiring their people in such a way that it causes an emotional effect. Fourth, provided that the leader is convincing, followers will want to be part of the operation and work towards the common goal themselves. This process is one of alignment. It is similar to stroking iron filings with a magnet: people are magnetised towards the same direction by the prospect of the vision becoming reality.

Fifth, effective leaders bring out the best in people. This involves a holistic approach which embraces motivation, empowerment, coaching and encouragement. Sixth, leaders need to be proactive in a situation of continual change. In effect, they become change agents. The seventh attribute is the ability to make decisions in times of crisis and for the ambiguous.

These seven competencies, which are discussed in detail in our last book *The Business of Leadership*,[8] are the skills required to lead effectively at all levels, in the appropriate style, in order to add value to an organisation.

■ The leadership dilemmas of constant change

The competencies outlined above need to be tested against the essence of leadership today; the requirement to deal with complex issues in an environment of constant change. This combination of complexity and constant uncertainty produces really difficult dilemmas for today's leaders, at whatever level they are operating. In the research for this book, we have discussed the leadership dilemmas with individuals working at the operational, team and strategic levels. The following summary includes a review of the main issues which were raised with us. No attempt has been made to distinguish whether a particular dilemma is more of an issue at any specific level: indeed, the changing shape of organisations suggests that the boundaries are becoming increasingly blurred.

Flattening the organisation

Probably the most fundamental issue is the movement in organisations from hierarchies to flatter structures. This has led to an increased span of control – and of responsibility. For instance, in Honda Cars UK there are only five levels from the managing director downwards. Although these developments have provided a fitting challenge to those individuals who have been elevated to higher levels of management, many have assumed these extra responsibilities with insufficient time to acquire the necessary experience. Not surprisingly, there have been a number of casualties, which has adversely affected both the individual and the organisation. The other effect of the movement towards flatter structures has been the implications for bureaucracy. This is a characteristic of large organisations, however: as they have changed shape, so they have tried to cope without the old systems which were thought to be too cumbersome and slow for today's technological age. The problem is that the new organisations have discovered that it is difficult to survive without some form of control system.

Old and new

The next dilemma is also associated with the differences between 'old' and 'new' – but this time it is associated with age: it is the knowledge 'age-gap'. The advances in technology in the past decade have been quite astonishing – particularly those associated with the computer. Whilst the older generation have tried to adapt to this change (with mixed success), the young have grown up with the computer and have therefore acquired the necessary skills quite naturally. This has threatened those in management positions, particularly at the senior level, because they are not sufficiently competent in this area. This is just a passing phase as, over the next few years, all of us will develop the necessary skills. However, for those currently aged forty and above who are in senior management, this has proved to be a significant problem which, in some cases, has affected their behaviour.

Technology

Technology is also the source of the next problem area – that of leading *ad hoc* and remote teams. Due to the pressures of business, a number of problems are tackled by project teams which are brought together for a short period, varying from a few weeks to a number of months. The difficulty with this arrangement is that, quite often, the team is *ad hoc* and its members have not operated together before. This poses a particular leadership problem – as does the requirement to lead a team that does not meet for days and, in some circumstances, for weeks. This is becoming increasingly common as more people undertake part of their work from home, or are away from the office for long periods. These circumstances are proving to be particularly difficult for leaders who have been used to daily contact which, in turn, has enabled them to develop a close relationship with their teams.

Empowerment

Empowerment brings with it all sorts of dilemmas. The openness and accountability, which is a strong feature of empowerment, provides for effective leadership at all levels and it is based on trust. However, that trust has to be complete, with no doubts between the individuals involved in the relationship. The same applies with 'openness' – it is not possible to be 'half-open'. This raises difficulties with regard to areas of confidentiality. For example, the members of a company board locked in difficult discussions about a possible merger are not able to discuss the details with their workforce. However, this reticence may be interpreted wrongly by the employees which, in turn, may undermine their trust with the board. Empowerment also implies a sharing of information as well as responsibility. The problem is that some people do not want to share the former, and others do not want to accept the latter!

This whole area is associated with a move towards a more democratic style of management. In effect, 'empowerment' involves a sharing of power. This raises some tricky issues, such as, who is the actual leader? How do you operate the necessary control measures? How much do you need to exercise control?

The movement towards a more democratic style, together with the faster pace of life, has led to an increasing overlap between the strategic and the operational levels of leadership. Those operating at the operational level need to understand the whole picture; whilst those at the strategic level need to appreciate the operational implications. Constant dialogue between the two levels is essential if organisations are going to be able to react fast enough in today's world.

Significantly, the British Armed Forces are particularly good at managing the strategic/operational communications overlap. Experience of three decades of operations in Northern Ireland have taught the British Army and the Royal Marines the importance of every soldier understanding the political environment in which they have to operate. This is achieved by daily briefings, supplemented by instant updates over the military radio net when necessary, to keep everybody up to date with events. Similarly, senior officers are constantly reminded about the practical implications of their decisions during their frequent visits to the troops on the ground. The benefits of this procedure were again evident when British soldiers were interviewed on television on the streets of Pristina in summer 1999, as part of NATO's peacekeeping force in Kosovo.

Managing the workload

The final issue concerns that of the increasing workload. It has been estimated that stress is costing the UK in excess of £26 billion per annum.[9] The time pressures on all of us are enormous, and the global market means that many businesses never stop. The trouble with that is that the people who work for those businesses have to work round the clock as well. All this pressure impacts on the work/home balance.

All of the issues discussed above have forced a significant rethink about leadership. Although a number of these dilemmas have occurred in the past, it is the relentless pressure of leading in an environment of continual change which has forced so many people to review how they live their lives. Is it really worth working 80 hours a week year after year, if I do not see my family growing up? If empowerment is meant to spread the levels of responsibility and workload, why am I suffering from stress? If this pressure is going to continue for the rest of my working life, do I have the energy to continue at this level until I reach retirement age? And, incidentally, at what age do I retire?

Although many people today are excited by the challenges of tackling complex issues and leading people through the chaos of uncertainty, others are questioning the very basis of leadership and responsibility. This questioning is set against a background of a portfolio lifestyle and different patterns of work. For instance, according to The Henley Centre study commissioned by Barclays Bank, 2020 *Vision Report*,[10] we are moving towards a world where it will be normal to work for just four days a week, with the fifth day spent on voluntary work. There will also be more time for leisure.

Most people in leadership roles today do not recognise such a world and are only just surviving under the mounting pressures of meeting quicker deadlines with fewer and fewer resources. No wonder the more talented are taking extended breaks from their jobs.

Developing intellectual capital

So what of leadership in the future? What will be the focus of the leader in the new millennium where the challenges and demands on business leaders are even greater than they have been in the twentieth century? We believe the focus of most business leaders will shift from developing just the physical asset base of their organisations (such as the plant value, the inventory and buildings) towards a true recognition of the knowledge and intellectual capital contained within the business or organisation. Leif Edvinsson and Michael Malone[11] have addressed this issue in a most comprehensive way in their book.

These authors argue that every organisation contains a tremendous amount of knowledge both in its computer and information technology systems. In the past, accountants tended to value this aspect of the business as 'goodwill', a sort of vague valuation of the difference between the asset value of a business and the amount of money for which it could be sold in the marketplace. What we now have come to recognise is that a major component of that 'goodwill' factor is indeed the intellectual capital of the business, the value of the knowledge, skills and experience of both its people and its information systems. Leaders in the future will have to pay more attention to developing this aspect of the organisation than they have in the past. The future is about information, communication, knowledge and people. And those are the prime components of intellectual capital which, increasingly, will become the true measure of the value of an enterprise.

■ Summary

The realities of constant change have exposed a number of dilemmas that are affecting the very nature of leadership. The challenge has never been greater due to the pace of change and the tendency towards a more democratic approach. Being a leader today requires more subtle skills than in the past and a different emphasis, as organisational cultures change. The movement is from a 'comfortable' command and control approach to an 'uncomfortable' requirement to be an empowerer, a coach, a facilitator and an educator.

This is a difficult transition with which not everyone is happy. It implies more thought, greater flexibility, more anticipation and less direct control than in the past. The practicalities of this development will be addressed in the chapters that follow.

Endnotes

1   John Adair (1989), *Great Leaders*, Talbot Adair Press
2   Norman Dixon (1976), *On the Psychology of Military Incompetence*, Jonathan Cape
3   Leon Festinger (1957), *A Theory of Cognitive Dissonance*, Row Petersen
4   Ralph Stogdill (1974), *Handbook of Leadership*, Macmillan
5   Fred Fiedler *et al.* (1976) *Improving Leadership Effectiveness: The Leader Match Concept*, Wiley
6   Ken Blanchard and Paul Hersey (1969), *Management of Organizational Behavior*, Prentice-Hall
7   Philip Sadler (1997) *Leadership*, Kogan Page
8   Alan Hooper and John Potter (1997), *The Business of Leadership*, Ashgate
9   Neil Hartley (1996), *Towards a New Definition of Work*, London: RSA
10 The Henley Centre (1998) *2020 Vision*, London: Barclays Life 1998
11 Leif Edvinsson and Michael S. Malone (1997) *Intellectual Capital*, Piatkus

Appetiser

CHAPTER FOUR

In this chapter, you will:

■ START TO QUESTION YOUR ORGANISATION CHART

■ UNDERSTAND HOW MACHO LEADERSHIP AND SHORT-TERMISM CAN LEAD ORGANISATIONS INTO TROUBLE

■ GAIN AN INSIGHT INTO HOW SOME LEADERSHIP CHALLENGES HAVE BEEN HANDLED IN REAL ORGANISATIONS

■ DISCOVER SOME SPECIFIC KEYS TO SUCCESSFUL CHANGE LEADERSHIP

■ IDENTIFY THE RESPONSE PHASES EXPERIENCED BY INDIVIDUALS FACED WITH CHANGE

■ SEE THAT MORALE VARIES IN A PREDICTABLE WAY DURING A CHANGE PROGRAMME

■ FIND OUT MORE ABOUT REAL CASE STUDIES ON SUCCESSFUL CHANGE LEADERSHIP

■ DISCOVER WAYS TO SUSTAIN A SUCCESSFUL CHANGE PROGRAMME.

Responding to Change

■ The real world

It was a surprisingly warm day for October in Milton Keynes. We were at Volkswagen Group UK Ltd trying to understand the organisational chart.

'So, the headquarters is not represented as such, but instead it is reflected as functional departments operating as separate satellites in the outer ring.'

' Precisely.'

'But where do you appear on this diagram?' we asked Richard Ide, the Managing Director.

'I don't.'

'I don't follow you. Are you telling me that as Managing Director you do not appear on the organisation chart at all. Surely, this is complete abrogation of your responsibility?'

'Quite the opposite,' replied Ide. 'As I do not make any decisions, it is not appropriate for my position to appear on the chart.'

'But, if you don't make any decisions – who does? And what do you do?'

'The decisions are made by the brands (i.e., Volkswagen, Audi, etc.). As for my role, it is to create the right atmosphere to give other people the confidence to make the decisions.'

This discussion[1] with the Managing Director of a global company is all the more surprising as Richard Ide had been a self-confessed command and control leader for most of his forty-five years in the car business. Hardly surprising, since that had been the culture in the business for most of his working life. Indeed, most organisations are led by powerful, ambitious and egotistical CEOs who, by their behaviour, will have a direct impact on how a company responds to change – for good or ill.

We shall return to the Volkswagen story and Richard Ide's transformation later in the chapter, but the general point about CEO behaviour is critical in today's environment of constant change, technological revolution and changing patterns of work. There is growing evidence that the companies who have learnt how to cope with change successfully have created clear blue water between themselves and the rest of the competition.

In this chapter we will consider the issues, and will then go on to look at the keys to success, drawing on examples from both the private and the public sectors.

■ The issues

The first issue is that of 'macho leadership'. This is a common feature amongst CEOs, so many of whom are driven by ambition and a burning desire to achieve. Linked with this is a fear of failure which makes it difficult for them to admit mistakes. If the culture of the organisation is also an unforgiving one, it will reinforce the macho approach and make it even more difficult for people to learn from their mistakes. This applies both to those at senior management level and also those aspiring to reach the top. Such an environment makes it difficult to break the mould since the next generation of leaders tend to follow the role models at the top. This, in turn, cascades down through the company affecting the behaviour of the whole workforce.

The next issue is that of short-termism. This is related to the macho approach in that failure cannot be tolerated, especially in the context of a private company reporting to shareholders. The 'shareholder factor' has wrecked many a company, especially the smaller ones, because it forces the management to concentrate on the short-term results at the expense of the long-term vision. However, this is not confined to the private sector alone since politicians are continually faced with such dilemmas from their electorate.

The gradual recognition that the inclusive approach (involving all stakeholders – not just shareholders) is the important factor has forced a number of organisations to re-appraise their strategy and adopt a more long-term approach. However, so far only a relatively small number of companies have started to address this issue properly. When you are struggling to survive over the next few months it takes considerable courage to start a new strategy based on projected success in the future, at the expense of short-term loss. This is particularly true if the organisation is beyond the peak of performance and at Point B on the Sigmoid Curve (see Figure 4.1).

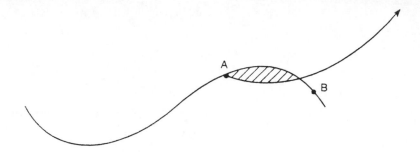

Figure 4.1 The Sigmoid Curve

This S-shaped curve represents the life cycle of an organisation which, inevitably waxes and wanes. The key is to start the second curve at Point A, before the peak, and thus use the latent energy of experience from the old curve whilst still at the development stage. The Sigmoid Curve is a particularly useful model with regard to timing. Get the timing right and you can use the down curve at the beginning of the new process (when you are still experimenting and learning – at Point A) before you reach the 'crest' of the old process. Get the timing wrong (Point B) and you will find it difficult to recover the lost ground. It is so much more difficult to change an organisational culture if the company is struggling against the competition and has lost its way, as Marks & Spencer discovered in 1998.

The third issue is the failure to adapt to change sufficiently quickly. The speed of change today is such that, unless an organisation anticipates likely events far enough ahead, it is unlikely to maintain the energy to keep up in an environment of constant change. This also means being comfortable with discontinuity. This last point is of particular relevance since it affects all kinds of bodies, from large private companies and public-sector organisations, to small companies with well-established reputations. Indeed, the better the reputation the more difficult it can be to live with discontinuity.

Take NATO. The most successful defence alliance in the history of the world which had kept the peace in Europe during the Cold War for over forty years, but yet found itself in real difficulty when faced with President Milosevic of Serbia in 1999, because he played to different rules. The tactics that had worked against a predictable opponent like the Soviet Union were no longer effective against an enemy who was prepared to learn from experience (Milosevic had absorbed the lessons from earlier setbacks in Bosnia) and who had assessed the weaknesses of the Alliance. In effect,

Milosevic had become sufficiently comfortable with discontinuity that he had turned it to his advantage.

As we watched the drama unfold daily on our television screens whilst NATO struggled with its dilemmas, many business leaders must have been drawing comparison with their own situations. If a high-tech organisation, which possessed overwhelming firepower and sophisticated communications, could be embarrassed and out-thought by the propaganda machine of a third-rate military nation, then a large company could easily lose out to a smaller, quick-thinking outfit which anticipated well, reacted faster and was comfortable in an environment of continuous change.

The fourth issue is that associated with failures at the top of organisations. At the beginning of 1999, in contrast to the United States, an unprecedented number of blue-chip companies in UK were without chairmen or chief executives. This resulted in newspaper headlines about 'leadership business crisis' – and nervousness in the City. At one stage, thirty out of the FTSE Top 100 were either without a leader or were actively seeking a replacement (these included Barclays Bank, Cable & Wireless, Rank, EMI and Reed Elsevier). Indeed, it took the Anglo-Dutch information company Reed Elsevier eleven months to find a new Chief Executive, and the board was in such disarray that two directors resigned in protest over the recruitment policy.

All of this led to an analysis about what was wrong with business leadership in Britain, a debate that is still going on. One of the initial aspects that was identified was that there was a distinction between management and leadership, and the realisation that, whereas the former had been good enough to guide companies through the slower pace of life in the 1980s, this was no longer sufficient for the uncharted waters of the twenty-first century. The only surprise was that it had taken organisations so long to come to this conclusion.

Another aspect associated with this particular problem is that of poor top team performance. This can be to due to lack of competence, personality clashes, poor behaviour or simply that the senior management is not pulling together as a team. An example of the latter occurred at Barclays Bank when Martin Taylor, the Chief Executive, resigned unexpectedly at the end of 1998. He had been recruited at the age of forty-one from Courtaulds Textiles plc (where he had also been the Chief Executive) with no banking experience, but with a clear mandate to sort out the problems at the bank – they had just

reported their worst results for 300 years. Within three years, profits were at

£2.08 billion, earnings per share were at a respectable 83.6p and, just as important, Barclays had become a good place to work with better communications and management systems. So, what went wrong? There were some fundamental mistakes, such as a trading loss of £250 million in Russia in 1998, but the heart of the problem was the entrenched opposition within the senior management to the new ideas that Taylor was trying to introduce to the bank. He had been brought in to introduce radical ideas and, to an extent, he had succeeded, at least in the early years.

But in order to succeed year after year, it requires a top management team to work closely together in an atmosphere of absolute trust. It has been said that Taylor took too long to bring in his own people, people he could rely on, and without this support behind him he was bound to fail. Whatever the reason, there was certainly a failure of teamwork at the senior management level and, in addition, Barclays lost a talented chief executive (who appeared to resign in frustration) – and they were prepared to pay £7 million (£2 million salary plus £5 million of shares after three years) to hire a successor, Mike O'Neill, an American banker. Ironically, he also resigned, but this time after being diagnosed with a serious heart problem (he only spent one day in the London office), and it took Barclays another five months after that to recruit Matt Barrett, the former head of the Bank of Montreal in July, 1999.

The Barclays example also highlights another failing amongst many organisations – that of failure to ensure proper succession planning. At the end of the 1990s Lonrho, GEC and Hanson all had problems with succession. This is often a symptom of 'macho leadership', a lack of empowerment and a failure to develop talent through appropriate coaching and mentoring. It is also a frequent outcome of the 'command and control' approach, which was the norm in the 1980s. Unfortunately, a large number of senior managers have found it very difficult to change from this style, especially when under pressure, with the result that either there has been no succession planning at all, or the talented have become disenchanted and left to join the opposition.

This failure in succession planning is part of the organisational culture issue which can cause considerable problems if it is not tackled properly. All companies have cultures which are specific to them. They are the result of the combination of the history of the organisation and the style of management which has developed over the years. The more successful the company, the more the prevailing culture is reinforced. In such circumstances it is very difficult for a new leader to change attitudes and behaviours. Sir Peter Davis found this to be the case when he took over as the Group Chief Executive of

Prudential Corporation in 1995: 'I was faced with a very conservative attitude when I first arrived here, based on the fact that the Prudential had been Britain's largest life insurance company for over a hundred years.'[2]

Apart from the normal difficulties associated with changing the culture of a single company must now be added those associated with takeovers and mergers, which have increased at an unprecedented rate at the end of the twentieth century, due to the increased competition of globalisation. For instance, the car industry has seen extensive change including the BMW acquisition of Rover, Ford of Volvo and the merger of Daimler-Benz with Chrysler.

Other industries have seen equally spectacular movement such as the British Aerospace merger with the Marconi Electronic System arm of GEC, and the Exxon-Mobil merger at the end of 1998 to make it the biggest oil company in the world. This followed the BP-Amoco merger in August that year, a company which then surprised everyone by proposing a deal with Arco in April 1999 with the aim of forming the world's second biggest oil company in April 1999. All of these alterations bring with them massive changes and considerable disruption to the cultures of organisations. It does not matter whether it is a takeover or a merger, the fundamental issue is to find the best method of getting people to develop an identity with and a loyalty for the new company. If empowerment and communications are difficult to achieve at the best of times, then it is even more difficult in such circumstances.

So far we have identified the major issues which companies have had to address when faced with change. These include: macho leadership; short-termism; failure to adapt sufficiently quickly; failure at the top; and organisational culture. Although this list is not definitive, it does embrace the major problems being faced by organisations today, problems which so many are finding frustratingly difficult to resolve. We will now move on to consider the keys to success, including an analysis of those organisations who appear to have discovered successful strategies.

■ Keys to success

During our research we discovered a number of companies who were managing change surprisingly well. They varied in size, they were spread across different industries and they were from both the private and the public sectors. Some of them had published what they were achieving, but most were too busy and too involved in what they were doing to have had time to reflect on their journey – for it was a journey they were on; a continual journey of constant change. Gary Hamel has referred to this as 'managing the marathon of continual change'.[3] He then went on to comment that not many were good at this.

But some are managing this process well, and we have had the good fortune to talk to some of them to discover what it is that they are doing right. We have analysed this, added our own thoughts on what are the key aspects, and brought all this together under relevant headings.

Complete cultural behavioural change

The first part of the process, which all the successful companies undertook, is a complete behavioural change which embraces everyone in the workforce – without any exceptions. The aim is to establish a set of values which not only places human behaviour at the heart of the culture, but also becomes the catalyst for encouraging leadership at all levels throughout the organisation. Honda have taken this even further with the development of the 'Honda Philosophy'. This was produced as a concise and readable pamphlet in 1992 by Nobuhiko Kawamoto, the President and CEO of the company. Significantly, he acknowledged the input from a number of Honda associates, particularly in Honda's larger markets, thus reflecting their international viewpoint. The philosophy starts with 'Fundamental beliefs' (which commences with 'Respect for the individual' – based on initiative, equality and trust) and then proceeds to 'Company principle' and 'Management policies'. It is perhaps significant that, in this eleven-page document, the word 'car' does not appear at all. Instead, there are much more interesting words – like 'joy', 'dreams' and 'a challenging spirit'. Just so that we are clear about the implications of such a philosophy, it has enabled Honda to survive the surprising decision of British Aerospace to sell Rover to BMW in 1994 rather than to Honda, and thus continue a successful fifteen-year partnership; and it also resulted in a return on investment in 1997, second only to Daimler-Chrysler.[4]

Another example from the car industry, that of Volkswagen Group UK Ltd, also illustrates the impact of behavioural change. The story starts at the beginning of the 1990s, just prior to the recession. At that time, the company was owned by Lonrho, but with a factory buy-out option (the company was acquired in 1973). Richard Ide, the Managing Director, realised that things were about to change in the car industry and that, in particular, VW's 'quality' position in the market was about to be challenged by cheaper competition. He also realised that Lonrho was likely to leave him alone in case VW exercised their option early. He therefore used this opportunity to do two things: cut costs; and put the company through a team and behavioural culture change programme.

The first priority was the cost-cutting exercise. This involved removing hierarchies (they reduced from seven levels down to three), outsourcing where other specialist companies had an expertise that VW could not match (i.e., TNT, AA, RAC and Unipart), and reducing the workforce from 1400 to 500. This took place over a four-year period from 1989–92 and was very hard work involving a lot of heartache and difficult decisions, but Ide knew that they were essential if the company was to be in the right shape to face the future with any degree of confidence. In parallel with the cost-cutting exercise, the company also ran a team and cultural change programme. This lasted two years (1991–92), was tailored to VW UK, and involved all 500 of the workforce, including the Managing Director.

This programme had a dramatic effect on behaviour within the company – it fundamentally changed the way people related to each other, and this included the behaviour of Richard Ide himself. In particular, it led to better listening skills, more open communication, more confidence – and therefore more autonomy. It enabled VW to radically change the way they were doing things which, in turn, has enabled them to remain very competitive in an extremely tough market. And, as we shall see later on in this chapter, the process is still continuing.

We have seen from this case that the Managing Director participated fully in the change programme. This is a fundamental requirement if such a programme is going to have any chance of success. The impact on the particular individual is likely to be marked, but it is the influence on the rest of the workforce which will be crucial. In another example, the authors facilitated a two-day team-building programme for the newly elected Heads of Schools at Exeter University in the summer of 1998, just prior to their taking up their new appointments. The university had just gone through a radical reorganisation which involved merging sixty-odd departments and centres into seventeen new multi-disciplinary schools, so the programme was an important part of the process.

As one can imagine, the organisational change was not popular with everyone, and therefore the new Heads of the Schools were going to need support and help, particularly in their first year. Hence the importance of this programme – and the role taken by the Vice-Chancellor, Sir Geoffrey Holland. He altered the original date chosen for the course because it clashed with another commitment which he was unable to change, he then attended the whole of the two-day programme, varying his participation so as not to inhibit others (especially in discussion). His contribution to the final discussion was significant in that he openly admitted the areas in which he personally could do better in the future. The impact on his new Senior Management Team was considerable, particularly in bonding them together at such an early stage.

It is clear from these two cases that the example from the top of an organisation is crucial in order to achieve behavioural change. Furthermore, since this is the beginning of the process, the behaviour of the senior management at this early stage assumes enormous significance. It needs to be recognised that it is not always easy for those at the top (many of whom will have been with the organisation for a number of years and will also probably be in their forties or fifties) to contribute wholeheartedly in such a programme. However, for those that approach this with some trepidation, they can take heart from Richard Ide who was in his early fifties when VW embarked on their programme and, at that stage, had been with the company for some thirty years.

It is also important that there is support from the whole of the organisation. The Training Group Defence Agency of the Royal Air Force embarked on an imaginative change programme in 1997 under their Chief Executive, Air Vice-Marshal Tony Stables. He set an excellent example by encouraging empowerment and urging his senior officers to release the creative talent of their people. The effect within the Agency was exhilarating as the various training establishments began to realise their true potential. 'A real feeling of trust began to develop throughout the organisation, and a number of people thanked me for giving them the opportunity.'[5] Unfortunately, this was not matched by the behaviour of those above Stables. There was suspicion amongst the top management. Ironically, this was largely based on the fact that the Agency was using management terminology which was alien to the Service environment at that time.

This was particularly ironic because the impressive results, with which the critics could not argue, were being achieved by good leadership – not by management. The outcome of this lack of support from the top management of the RAF was to restrict the pace of development, weakening effectiveness as the energy became too dissipated. As we shall see later on, this sustainability is one of the key performance indicators for assessing the effectiveness of 'change leadership'. Restructuring is a complex process and support from above is fundamental. It requires courage to press on without it; if there is opposition from above success is rarely achieved.

The last point to mention under this section is the use of facilitators during the behavioural change process. VW and the RAF used external help, whereas Exeter relied on in-house assistance. It does not matter which alternative is used, provided that the facilitators are experts – and that they are able to take an objective and detached view. Those who have relied on their internal resources have stressed the importance of the latter point, and have also warned against involving the Chief Executive, or his key senior managers, in this role. It is impossible to both facilitate the inevitable tensions that will occur on such a programme whilst at the same time trying to play a full part in the process, as a senior executive.

The behavioural culture change programme is the start of the process for transforming an organisation. It is hard work, it should not be underestimated – and it is essential. For the faint-hearted, take inspiration from Ford who, under their CEO (Jacques Nasser) put all 55,000 salaried employees through an intensive and integrated educational programme.[6]

It Takes Time!

Achieving success with change takes time. This simple fact, which is based on the experience of all those companies which have succeeded, seems to take by surprise a number of those about to embark on the journey. The fundamental reason for this is that a major transition process will challenge the beliefs and values of each individual. In order to adjust to change, individuals need to pass through the four stages illustrated in Figure 4.2: (1) denial – a refusal to acknowledge that change is necessary; (2) resistance – active opposition to change; (3) exploration – testing out various aspects of change; (4) commitment – a realisation of the benefits of change.

These phases are discussed in more detail in Chapter Five.

The majority of people will go through this full process as they seek to rationalise what they are being required to do. This is both an external and an internal process. Initially, they may hope that, if the problem is ignored, it will go away. This is the 'externalisation' of the change. However, as they

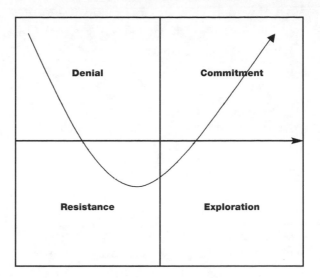

Figure 4.2. The four basic human response phases to change

progress through the process, individuals often 'internalise' it as they see the change as an increasing threat. Inevitably, all this takes time, indeed, it is important that it does because people need to be convinced of the benefits of going through such an experience – and they will need convincing again and again.

There are no half measures in this process. Those organisations which think that they can find a magic formula from some management book, tailor it to their requirements and then take some short cuts are in for a disappointment. All the lessons from the companies which are considered to be world class is that this takes time – and it is continuous. Take, for instance, BP. They started their cultural change programme in 1990 and moved from a position of eleven businesses and 120,000 people in the 1980s to three core businesses and 57,000 people by the end of the 1990s. BP's journey has involved moving from the traditional power and support systems of a hierarchy to a culture which involves little structure, sharing authority, coaching, cycling knowledge and constructive confrontation.[7] Much of this had been achieved before the merger with Amoco – and so their journey continues.

One of the other reasons that it takes so long is that change involves new ways of working, and also innovation. Companies are constantly looking for new ideas and for better methods of getting the best out of their people. This requires a certain energy from within the organisation which needs to be sustainable throughout the period of transition. This is illustrated in Figure 4.3.

This figure is related to Figure 4.2 in that it also traces the human responses to the various phases of the process (notice the scepticism and doubts at the beginning). Also note that there is no smooth ride of progress, but rather a series of 'ups and downs' as the organisation feels its way forward through uncharted waters. Also relevant is the importance of the leadership role in handling innovation.

How long will all this take? The model suggests 'up to two years', and the experience of companies who have gone through this process indicates that this is pretty accurate for the first stage (in effect, it continues for ever). Perhaps the best indicator is 'The Dark Night of the Innovator' which is right at the bottom of the curve. How do you know when you have reached there? Bitter experience suggests that when you believe that things cannot get worse and then they do – that is when you are there! As the reader will have realised by now, there is no science to all of this. Most of management is learnt by bitter experience, hence both the frustration and the fascination of it all.

It also involves a determination to see the change process right through, acknowledging that there will be a number of unexpected 'downs', especially at the beginning. This requires considerable resilience from the leaders, as well as an attitude of continual optimism and encouragement as they struggle with the inevitable setbacks. It also requires patience, not only because of the process, but also because of the effect on the people themselves. As Sir Geoffrey Holland put it: 'I could have introduced the changes more quickly, but this would probably have led to a build-up of resistance.'[8] The other reason for resilience is that there is no end to the process. We are now in the age of continuous change, and it means just that. If you look at all the organisations which are maintaining their position as world leaders, it is due to the fact that they have adjusted to the marathon. This applies equally to General Electric, as it does to BP Amoco, Honda, Ford or Xerox.

Adjusting to the time it takes to manage the change process takes anticipation and flexibility. It also requires an intelligent approach and a sensitivity to ensure that people are able to cope with the process. More and more organisations are realising that this is not straightforward and that it

Organisational responses to change

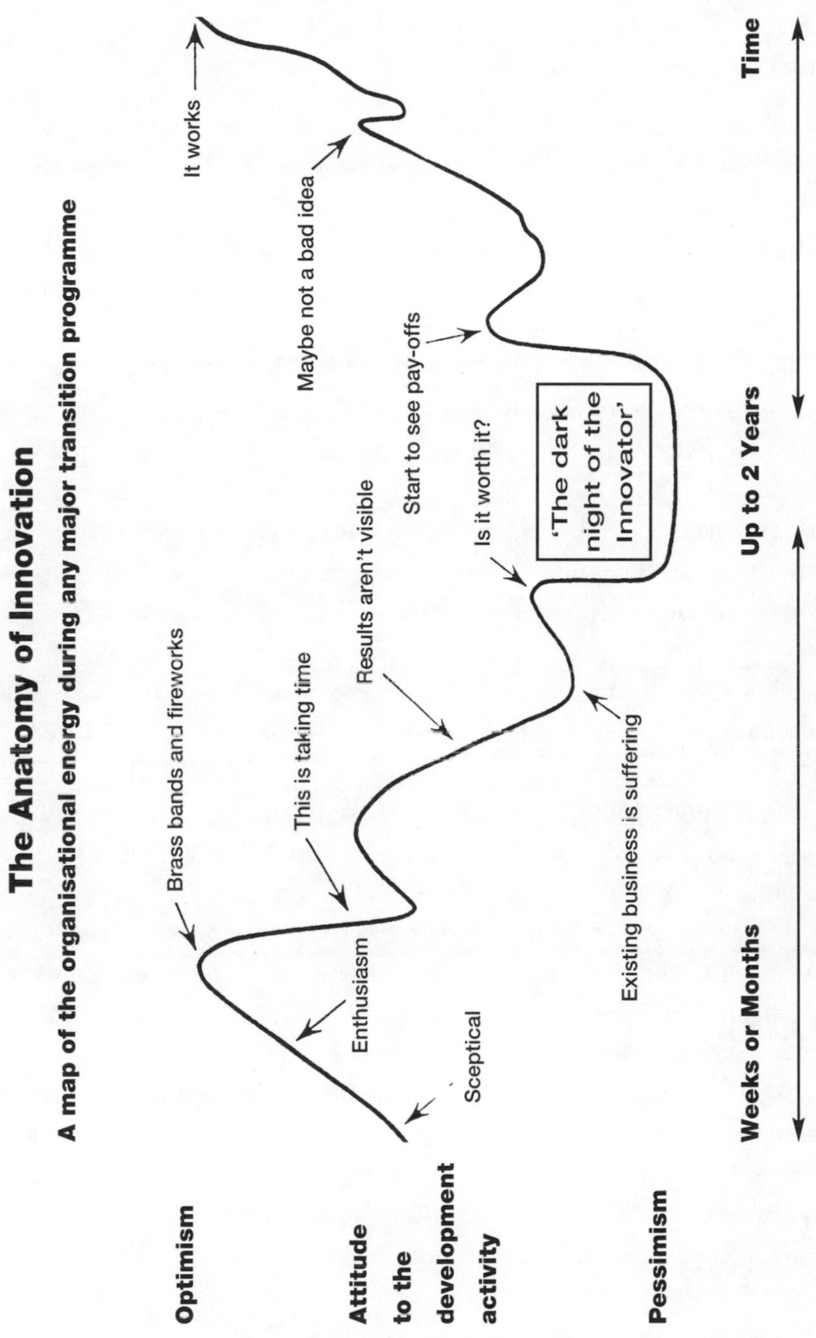

The Anatomy of Innovation

A map of the organisational energy during any major transition programme

Optimism

Attitude to the development activity

Pessimism

Brass bands and fireworks

Enthusiasm

Sceptical

This is taking time

Results aren't visible

Is it worth it?

Start to see pay-offs

'The dark night of the Innovator'

Maybe not a bad idea

It works

Existing business is suffering

Time

Weeks or Months   Up to 2 Years

Figure 4.3 The Anatomy of Innovation   85

requires some of the best brains, both inside and outside the organisation, to ensure that the optimum is achieved.

Good communications

When Archie Norman took over as the Chief Executive of Asda (the superstore chain) in 1991, the customers were drifting away, the share price was very low and the staff were despondent. Within four years he had turned it around so effectively that Asda had become the darling of the City. Norman had achieved this by liberating the workforce with imaginative management and a clear view on communications.

His approach embraced the full spectrum of this crucial area including an insistence that everyone referred to him as 'Archie', an active listening campaign (which included the 'Tell Archie' scheme that attracted 14,000 suggestions in the first eighteen months), and the introduction of the monthly board meetings in the stores during which time board members were expected to talk to about thirty-five people, both staff and customers. He also introduced the enterprising idea of the Asda baseball cap, to be worn by people who did not want to be talked to, because they needed two hours' thinking time. Interestingly, Norman never wore his own cap because he always wanted to be accessible at work. He did his thinking at home.

Norman developed an open communication policy which helped to unlock the potential of his workforce. His approach is particularly significant because he instilled a sense of pride and ownership amongst his people, despite the mundane nature of their work. Later on he introduced other ideas, such as the share option scheme, which were to cement the bond between him and the workforce even more strongly, but none of this would have happened without the trust that was developed as a result of the open communications. This openness was built on the fact that he always told it 'as it was'. There was no attempt to 'talk up' the situation at the beginning. Asda was in a mess, the employees knew it, Norman knew it, and he did not try to disguise it. Instead, he adopted a frank approach, especially during the early days of restructuring which, initially, won him grudging respect and then, subsequently, a growing momentum of support.

Norman also built around him a close-knit management team and ensured that he knew all the store managers (some 200). Another company, in an entirely different industry, have developed an innovative management structure specifically designed to make communications more effective.

Honda UK has a flat structure with just five levels from top to bottom. Their philosophy is based on the premise that teamwork is essential in a flat organisation. They are also clear that, in order to be effective, any communication system needs to provide for clear dissemination of information, both up and down, as well as a good process for listening. As Ken Keir, the Managing Director put it: 'It is important to create clear understanding at all levels.'[9] The combination of a team-based structure and a requirement for good communications has resulted in the organisational structure shown at Figure 4.4.

Notice that it is referred to as 'team' structure, thus emphasising what is really important in organisational terms. The system has a couple of rules which are significant: There should be no more than ten people in a team circle; and there should be one member who is in two circles, and it is their responsibility to provide the communication link between the two. With these two simple guidelines, Honda have developed a most effective structure which reinforces communications, rather than hinders it. It is also no accident that there is no hierarchical shape to it. Indeed, there is no 'shape', as such, at all. Also note that the management team includes the secretary as an equal member. Honda has developed a structure which is both symbolic and practical, based on their philosophy and evolved through experience.

In contrast to these two large companies, Wagadon, the magazine publishing company, employs only seventy-five full-time staff. However, its influence is considerable amongst the sixteen to twenty-five-year-olds, mainly through the monthly cult magazines *Arena* and *The Face*, with circulation figures of 68,000 and 79,000 respectively. The company is based in a large warehouse in North London, with a floor allocated to each of these magazines, in an open-plan environment.

The Editor of *Arena*, Ekow Eshun, has an office to one side, but is able to hear the soft music which plays constantly in the background. He is aged thirty, and at twenty-eight was the youngest person to be appointed to edit a men's magazine. He has not had a day's management training in his life but, despite this, appears to be doing most things right because of his understanding about the basics of communication and its importance in getting the best out of people: 'My role is to bring my own enthusiasm to the magazine and help people to feel proud to work for *Arena*. Working together as a team is very important – as is a shared vision, and a powerful sense of fun! The open atmosphere and relaxed environment aids communication which, in turn, helps with the creativity.'

TEAM STRUCTURE

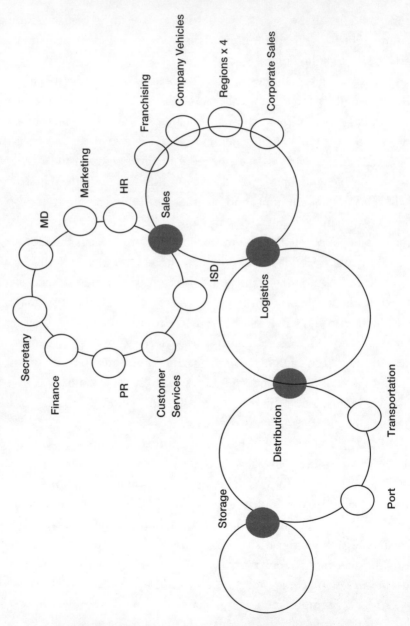

Figure 4.4 Honda UK team structure (reproduced by kind permission of the Managing Director, Honda UK)

This was echoed by Richard Benson, the Group Editor of Wagadon: 'It is important to nurture the talent of the young people who work here. That means being available, listening – and encouraging. It also involves finding ways of giving responsibility in small areas.'[10]

These two editors have applied common sense, followed their instincts and devised an approach to communications which has helped to unlock the creative talents of their people – and the result is two successful magazines. They have shown that there is nothing complicated in this provided that, first of all, you think about what you are doing, and then you set an example of behaviour which is founded on integrity. All of these issues are linked. Communication cannot be viewed in isolation. It is the connecting of these pieces together that provides part of the intellectual challenge.

In the context of this last comment, perhaps it is no accident that all bar one of the key individuals in all the cases quoted in this section have degrees. Indeed, Archie Norman not only has an economics degree from Cambridge, he also graduated from the Harvard Business School, and then became a management consultant with McKinsey & Co.

Empowerment

When Dennis Bakke, the CEO of AES Corporation (the world's largest power company), was asked in an interview with the *Harvard Business Review* whether he had set out to make the company an empowered one, he replied: 'We knew that we wanted to create a very different kind of company, that's for sure. I don't think we used the word "empowerment" – I'm not sure it was even around in 1981.'[11] That word has been so overused and misunderstood that there are many people who wish it had never been invented! It is almost as though the word itself has created a barrier; however, the basis of empowerment is straightforward. In the same interview Roger Sant, the Chairman and Founder of AES, explained: 'Our system starts with a lack of hierarchy. We abhor layers. We avoid them like the plague . . . So we organize around small teams . . . each containing about five to twenty people . . . We're moving toward a system in which each team has total responsibility for its area both in terms of operations and maintenance.'[12]

In these few simple phrases Sant has got to the heart of empowerment. It is all about a rejection of hierarchy in favour of small teams and responsibility. There seem to be two fundamental reasons why organisations find empowerment so difficult. The first is a reluctance to give up hierarchies; the second is a lack of determination to see the process right through to its conclusion. The latter requires considerable patience and an ability to adapt the process in the light of experience (it is significant that AES are still learning and adapting eighteen years after they started on their journey of empowerment).

The foundation of empowerment is values. We have already seen that this is the bedrock of organisational culture so it is not surprising to see its importance being highlighted again. Without a clear set of values there can be no trust, and without trust there can be no empowerment. This is evident from the companies which we have already looked at, such as AES, Asda and Honda; and it is particularly true of Levi Strauss. In an interview with *Management Today*, Haas (the Chief Executive) stressed that the company had always tried to conduct business in ways that were consistent with their values, which included recognition for those who contributed to their success: 'Motivated employees are our source of innovation and competitive edge.'[13]

Levi Strauss went even further by extending that recognition to a reward scheme which involved a commitment in June 1996 to pay all the 37,000 employees one year's salary as a bonus to celebrate the new millennium – payable in 2002. Inevitably there were strings attached to this attractive scheme, including a cumulative net cash flow of $7.6 billion by the end of the financial year 2001 (which was considered attainable). But the significance of this initiative was the transparent faith which the management had in their workforce. It was all about ownership and sharing – and it had an immediate impact.

Even when the company had to fire a third of its employees a year later, it was made clear that those who had been made redundant would still be eligible for the bonus, as well as being given eight months' notice and receiving help to find a new job. Haas believed that, despite the redundancy programme, the generous severance package would help those left behind: 'Our people will know that, if bad times happen, then they will be treated much better than they would have elsewhere.'[14] Levi Strauss had been generous when they were doing well, and their CEO believed that they should be just as fair when they were not doing so well. This will be put to the test over the next couple of years, given the announcement in March 1999 that the 1998 sales had dropped 13%.

In discussing values, we have also mentioned ownership. In order for empowerment to work there has to be a real sense of ownership amongst the employees. We have already seen how this has been achieved at Asda, and it

has also been developed most effectively at John Lewis Partnership, the twenty-five-branch department store and 120-branch Waitrose supermarket chain. Spedan Lewis inherited the successful John Lewis department store business his father had founded in Oxford Street, but transferred his interest to a trust for the benefit of the workforce (Partners), believing that their investment was as crucial to success as finance and that they should therefore share the profits. This was remarkably far-sighted for the early years of this century, when even today few businesses would be ready to equate their employees' importance with that of their shareholders. However, it is strange that the real benefit of such an approach has not been realised by more organisations.

As a result of Spedan Lewis' decision sixty years ago, in 1999 the 40,000 Partners who worked for John Lewis and Waitrose shared an £81m profit bonus. As Sir Stuart Hampson, the Chairman, put it: 'Ownership has to mean something.' He also went on to say: 'Happiness is a fundamental objective of management. People need a sense of fulfilment, a feeling of satisfaction. If they are happy at work, then they are more likely to give of their best.'[15] This linkage of ownership, happiness and profit-sharing provides a transparency which is crucial if ownership is really to mean something. Hampson keeps happiness on the agenda by interviewing his top sixty managers to find out what they are doing about it.

Another good example of ownership comes from Volkswagen Group UK. We have already seen how they went through a radical behavioural change, and heard that Richard Ide is a strong believer in empowerment. The result of all the thinking that went on within the company during the cultural change process in the early 1990s led to the realisation that the organisational structure itself needed to be altered. This stemmed from the acknowledgement that it was difficult to be good at everything. 'So, if you want to be really good, then empower people and allow them to become good in their own fields.'[16] With this philosophy in mind the senior management group, consisting of some eighty people, met for a day in 1994 to devise a new autonomous structure. The end result was the diagram shown in Figure 4.5.

This planning exercise to devise the new structure provides an excellent example of ownership – and the resulting diagram is a first-class picture of empowerment. It is based on the premise that the important decisions are those made by the brands (Audi, Skoda, VW, etc.) and therefore they are the largest satellites in the VW Group UK area of responsibility. They, in turn, relate inwards to each of their customers via their dealers (each brand has a different type of customer), and outwards to the specialist outsources (AA,

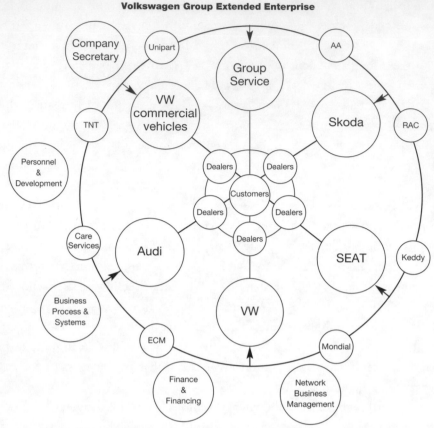

Figure 4.5 Volkswagen Group extended enterprise (reproduced by kind permission of the Managing Director, Volkswagen Group UK Ltd)

RAC, TNT, Unipart, etc.) and also to the relevant department of the 'head office' (business process & systems, personnel & development, etc.). Head office provides the link with Volkswagen AG. As we noticed at the beginning of the chapter, the Managing Director does not appear in the diagram at all, and the idea of a 'head office' is deliberately diffused by its representation in the structure in the form of functional departments only.

It is a remarkably transparent diagram of empowerment. It is perhaps significant that, although the thought process was started in 1994, it was another three years before the diagram was actually drawn. The strength of the system is highlighted by the fact that the behaviour of empowerment is extended to Volkswagen AG. The CEO has never phoned Richard Ide during his time as Managing Director (he has trusted the relationship which has developed between Ide and his Main Board member). Even the latter only phones him three or four times a year.

This is what ownership is all about. It is fundamentally dependent on the behaviour of the leadership at the top of the organisation – and that is the key to empowerment. Although Richard Ide had developed his style before Dr Ferdinand Piech took over as the Chairman of Volkswagen Group Worldwide, their approach to management was the same: trust, ownership and empowerment – and this was reflected in their behaviour.

When they first met in 1993, Piech used a delightful phrase which summed up his attitude: 'You are as free as you are good.'[17] Something similar was said to one of the authors by his Brigade Commander as he was about to assume command of a Royal Marines Commando. It had the effect of communicating great trust which resulted in significant confidence at the moment of taking over a highly responsible job. One of the most important roles of a top leader is to boost the confidence of their senior management team, especially those in a leadership role. Leaders need support if they, in turn, are to develop an atmosphere of confidence within their organisations.

This behaviour influences everything – and it needs to be consistent. For instance, no one has an office at VW. This reinforces the philosophy of open communications, trust and a culture which places no emphasis on status and privilege. Ide has a 'space' just inside the door of the open-plan environment, only ten feet from his secretary's desk. In another motor company, Honda, the Managing Director is on the same 'package' as his secretary (including a company car). Asda, Honda and Mitel (the telecommunication company based in South Wales) all have meeting rooms in their companies which can be used by anyone. These are the source of creativity where ideas are developed and innovation is sparked, from specialist teams as well as the senior management.

All of the leaders at the top of these organisations set an example of consistent behaviour day after day after day. They know that this is crucial if they are to release the full potential in their people. Bakke of AES stressed the importance of this when he talked about the difficulty of getting leaders to: 'freely and consistently give up the power to make decisions. There are life-and-death decisions in our work all the time . . . But empowerment makes it safer – not riskier. If a team feels it is fully accountable, it will take more responsibility than if it feels that its boss is accountable.'[18]

All organisations which have really developed empowerment have learned to move from a command and control leadership style to one of coaching, facilitating and support. Those that have achieved this are moving further and further ahead of those organisations which have not.

■ Sustaining the change

A number of companies have managed to make progress on the key success factors discussed above, but have still not been able to manage the change process well. This has largely been because they have not been able to sustain it over a long period of time. In order to achieve this it is necessary to develop an approach which enables the organisation to be comfortable with discontinuity. This is not easy, especially for a body which has existed for a long time, evolved a culture over a number of years – and has been successful. It involves a 'challenging' ethos and a constant restlessness to continually improve. The Mars Group has such an ethos, and it is developed in their people from the day that they join the company (they know that maintaining their market lead depends on their ability to continually innovate). It also implies a constant desire to challenge accepted wisdom and to change the rules of the game.

In an article for *Fortune Magazine*,[19] Gary Hamel pointed out that top companies thrive on such an approach, and illustrated this with examples from Coca-Cola, Harley-Davidson, Nike and Nokia. This challenging approach is a crucial leadership role and one that needs to be adopted if an organisation is to have any hope of success. It is one of the reasons why the leadership at the top of an organisation often has to be changed before any real progress is made.

Another factor demonstrated by those that are succeeding is the ability to anticipate. Although this is a normal management requirement, it assumes a new meaning in today's environment of continual change. Now it means predicting what the future will be, and then taking the anticipatory measures to meet that future with the right answers. An example of this is Prudential's launch of its new direct-banking initiative in 1998 called 'Egg'. It was an inspired idea from what had been a traditional insurance company that directly challenged the old retail banking world in UK which, until recently, had only been serviced by the Big Four banks.

Underpinning the challenging ethos and anticipation are three core ingredients: integrity; a commitment to developing people; and a team culture. A high level of integrity is evident in all the most successful organisations. It stems from the example of their leaders (which will be discussed further in Chapter Six), and is founded on honesty and openness. Time and again these simple words kept recurring during our research. Those companies which were succeeding had a very open approach, both to their employees and to their customers. They were also extremely trusting and would often share sensitive information which could be of use to their competitors. This unassuming approach was in contrast to the less successful organisations who often appeared to be paranoid about the opposition.

The honesty would often be reflected in admitting mistakes. Indeed, this is a good test of honesty. It is not only the first step that an organisation is being honest with itself, it can also be the beginning of a new relationship with the 'customer'. Such an event occurred when Sir Paul Condon, the Commissioner of the Metropolitan Police, apologised to Stephen Lawrence's parents in October 1998 for the police's failure to catch the black teenager's killers. This came in the wake of the Inquiry by Sir William Macpherson which produced evidence of incompetence by those policemen who were involved in this tragic incident.

Although there was a great deal of anger and emotion surrounding this affair, which continued after the Inquiry Report was produced the following February, the admission by Condon encouraged the general public to believe that there was a determination from the top of the Metropolitan Police to change the culture of the Service. For an organisation to sustain change, honesty is often an essential first step.

Developing people is another essential ingredient. The difference between those companies which are really forging ahead and those which are stagnating is a strong commitment to their people. Time and again we came across companies who said that they valued their employees but whose actions did not match their words. They had limited training programmes, they did not undergo any development training themselves, and they cancelled the training and development budget at the first sign of a financial crisis. Not only did the latter occur during the Recession at the beginning of the 1990s but, unbelievably, this happened again in the summer of 1998 when, for a couple of months, it looked as though the financial downturn in Asia would have serious worldwide implications. Whilst caution was understandable, a surprising number of companies in UK had still not resurrected their training budgets a year later.

World class organisations have no such short-term approach to the development of their people. They have a strong commitment to providing learning opportunities for all their employees so that each individual has the chance the grow to their full potential. For instance, a number of companies have their own universities, such as Unipart and British Aerospace; Stage-coach have developed a learning facility which is available to everyone; and

GEC's Management College is spearheading the company's initiative to become a 'learning organisation' by adopting an anarchical approach, which involves both formal and informal programmes, designed to break down the functional barriers.

This commitment to people is underlined by the behaviour by the leaders at the top. When asked what kept him awake at night, a one-time Permanent Secretary from Whitehall replied that it was not the policy decisions that worried him the most; it was dilemmas about people that preoccupied him. Had he chosen the right person for promotion? Would a particular individual be well suited to a specific appointment? Such a priority is not restricted to the public sector. The Managing Director of Honda UK spends three to four hours per week with his Head of Human Resources talking about his people. This focus on his people has reaped its reward: 'I now have a young team which is operating at senior management level most successfully.'[20]

The commitment also embraces the creation of challenging appointments both to stretch the talented and also to discover how good they really are. This is linked with succession planning, which should be second nature to organisations but, alas, is not the case, even with some of the good companies. Developing intellectual capital is another aspect which the best companies are doing. As the world becomes more complicated, now that we are entering the Knowledge Age, world class companies are investing a considerable amount in recruiting and then developing the individuals with capacity to really learn. Some of them are blessed with good brains, others are less intellectually gifted, but compensate for this with a determination to learn. Organisations need both if they are to succeed in the future. Some, like BP, have been doing this for years.

The final aspect is that of developing a team culture. Too many companies have failed because the decisions have been left in the hands of one person – the chief executive. Time and again the elevated and isolated position of the CEO has resulted in crucial decisions being taken by one person, with little or no consultation. It is difficult to see how this can still occur, given all the talk about empowerment and the increasing movement towards a more democratic style of management. And yet, perhaps it is to be expected, given the egotistical driver which motivates a high number of people at the top of organisations. For it is the behaviour of the CEO which is the key to the culture of a company. If they are not interested in developing a team approach, then it will not happen. Interestingly, an increasing number of chief executives have deliberately given up their power and status in order to encourage a team approach. They have done this, largely, for pragmatic reasons for they have realised that this is the best way to keep their better people, as well as coming up with the clever solutions which, increasingly, are essential for success.

This is also a good means of developing a strategic approach within the company which concentrates on the long term and welds together a committed group of people who are dedicated to adapting to continuous change. It is also a good way of building succession from within the organisation, rather than having to rely on outside talent.

Further down the company, the team ethos is just as important. Although an increasing number have realised this and are practising it, few have taken the logical step of rewarding teamwork, rather than the individual.

The advantages of this team approach is evident in the whole ethos of the Japanese companies, and in Levi Strauss. The virtue of developing internal leaders is exemplified by the success of Jack Welch at General Electric and a succession of good CEOs at BP. The wasted energy of not coaching internal candidates for the top job is evident from what happened at Barclays. Not only did they recruit Martin Taylor from outside, but when he suddenly resigned, there was no-one waiting in the wings to succeed him.

In this respect, the public sector would appear to have a better system. Not only do they focus on the team approach, they also endeavour to run at least two candidates for the top job — at least this is true of the British Armed Services. Somewhat surprisingly, the one who fails to get the top job tends not to resign but, instead, serves on as the number two or in another capacity. This is due to the fact that there is a realisation in the Forces that the team is always more important than the individual. This suggests that the top organisations really understand what is meant by a team ethos. It is ingrained deep in their culture.

■ Summary

In this chapter we have looked at the issues that companies have to address when facing up to a constantly changing environment. These have included: 'macho leadership'; short-termism; failure to adapt sufficiently quickly; failure at the top; and organisational culture. Furthermore, this examination has revealed that there is a widening gap between those organisations that are managing change well, and those that are not.

In considering the 'keys to success' from the examples drawn from those companies which are doing well we have seen that the essential first part of the process consists of a complete cultural behavioural change. This is value-based, is a continual process and is dependent upon complete commitment from the top. The second ingredient is open communications. This is based on trust, with the emphasis on teamwork, and there is a determined effort to unlock the creative talents of people within the company. Furthermore, the most effective companies have restructured themselves so that their procedures positively help improve communications, rather than hinder them.

The third aspect centres on empowerment. Once again, it is based on shared values which, in turn, are transferred into ownership. There is a rejection of hierarchy, and this is reinforced by the behaviour and the example set by those at the top of the organisation. The fourth and final aspect is the ability to sustain the change. This requires considerable resilience from the leadership at the top, as well as an ability to anticipate. It also requires a 'challenging' ethos and consists of three core ingredients: integrity; a commitment to develop people (and thereby 'intellectual capital'); and a team culture.

Underpinning all of this is the behaviour of 'the leader'. This is essential for successful change management and requires:

- moral courage
- integrity
- an ability to really listen
- a readiness to admit mistakes
- trust
- consistency.

None of this is easy. But then, neither is leading change. However, provided that leaders set good examples, extraordinary changes can be achieved because this gives confidence to everyone in the organisation to really contribute.

One more thing. We may have given the impression throughout this chapter that 'change is good for you'. It may or it may not be: however, this is beside the point because the lesson from those companies which are tackling change so effectively is that they have seized the initiative and become masters of their own destiny. They have realised that the future is one of constant change, and have adapted accordingly. That is the underlying difference between the best companies and the rest.

Endnotes

1 Interview with Richard Ide, 6 January 1999

2 Interview with Sir Peter Davis, 13 January 1999

3 Institute of Personnel and Development Conference, Harrogate, England, 29 October 1998

4 *The Economist*, 13 February 1999

5 Interview with Air Vice-Marshal Tony Stables, 2 February 1999

6 *Harvard Business Review*, March–April 1999

7 Kate Owen in *Brathy Conference Report*, May 1998

8 Interview with Sir Geoffrey Holland, 7 January 1999

9 Interview with Ken Keir, 7 October 1998

10 Interview with Richard Benson and Ekow Eshun, 26 January 1999

11 *Harvard Business Review*, January–February 1999

12 *Ibid.*

13 *Management Today*, November 1996

14 *The Economist*, 8 November 1997

15 Interview with Sir Stuart Hampson, 25 June 1998

16 Richard Ide, *op. cit.*

17 *Ibid.*

18 *Harvard Business Review*, January–February 1999

19 *Fortune Magazine*, 23 June 1997

20 Ken Keir, *op. cit.*

Appetiser

CHAPTER FIVE

In this chapter, you will:

■   FIND OUT MORE ABOUT THE IMPACT OF CHANGE ON INDIVIDUALS AND HOW THEY REACT

■   DISCOVER MORE ABOUT WHAT MAKES PEOPLE TICK AT THE INDIVIDUAL AND GROUP LEVELS

■   LEARN HOW TO DEVELOP HUMAN PERFORMANCE BY CREATING THE CULTURE IN YOUR ORGANISATION, AND NURTURING THE PHYSICAL AND MENTAL STATE OF YOUR PEOPLE

■   BECOME MORE AWARE OF WAYS TO HANDLE RESISTANCE TO CHANGE AND GAIN COMMITMENT TO NEW WAYS OF DOING THINGS.

The Human Factor

■ The real impact of change at the human level

There is no doubt in anybody's mind that our organisations have undergone a tremendous transition in recent years. Most have downsized in order to become more efficient and embraced a level of information technology hitherto undreamed of. Furthermore, they seem to have become less sympathetic in terms of how they deal with employees. The idea of the family business with a job for life now seems to be a thing of the past. Yet at the same time as this streamlining process has been taking place, we have seen the growth of the Human Resource function, staff appraisals, development and training and a whole host of literature which seems to suggest that the emphasis in organisations is shifting from the so-called hard issues to the soft ones – from simply making a profit to caring for your people.

We read continually of organisations placing more value on the skills and knowledge of their people and their intellectual capital, rather than tangible assets. However, many individuals do not feel valued by their organisations. Perhaps those worst affected are the survivors following a downsizing and redundancy programme. This is the 'Survivor Syndrome' we mentioned earlier in the book. Whilst there are obvious problems for those individuals who are let go by the organisation, the effect on the survivors of under-mining confidence is often profound. Individuals often feel they have to work a lot harder just to avoid losing their positions in the organisation. It is no wonder that stress in the workplace is on the increase, particularly in the established organisations which traditionally have been 'safe havens' with secure career prospects.

The public sector, for example, often attracts individuals who are prepared to sacrifice short-term income for quality of life, a chance to contribute to society and job security. Yet in recent times, we have seen many public-sector organisations become leaner in terms of staff numbers, and not all of this reduction of headcount is through so-called natural wastage through retirement, job changes and the other normal reasons for people leaving the organisation. For many, it seems, the word 'change' is synonymous with the word 'threat'. And this is the fundamental challenge to the leader. How do you ensure that your people see change as an opportunity and a challenge rather than as a problem and a threat? To explore this issue we need to become aware of how people see 'change'. We also need to understand what makes people tick.

■ Understanding what makes people tick

Successful change leadership takes place at the level of the individual. Any leader set on the idea of creating effective change needs to understand how people view the world and their place in it and, in particular, how they see themselves in the organisational setting.

Over the years, there have been many attempts to create an effective model of the human being which will lead to a better understanding of the nature of motivation. One of the most useful approaches is one which has emerged from the field of Neuro-Linguistic Programming. Robert Dilts was the originator of the idea of this way of thinking about the human being. Two Englishmen, John Seymour[1] and John Potter, one of the authors of this book, then added additional thoughts to the original ideas. The model is shown in Figure 5.1 and is based on the idea that at the core of every individual is their sense of identity and, in some cases, a link with either a spiritual level or some other sense of higher purpose. Identity is seldom an absolute issue in terms of fact. It is more a perception. For example, the vast majority of terrorists will never call themselves by that label. Instead they would almost certainly refer to themselves as 'freedom fighters' or 'soldiers'.

So what makes the difference? It has to be in the area of beliefs. A professional fraudster may see himself or herself as a business person, whilst the authorities and the law see them as a criminal. The distinction is the set of beliefs which are different. Closely coupled with beliefs are values – what is important to an individual in terms of the way they exist on a daily basis. We can represent these ideas on a diagram (see Figure 5.1). Surrounding the identity level of how the individual sees himself are a set of beliefs and a set of values. It is difficult to say whether beliefs or values is the area closer to the

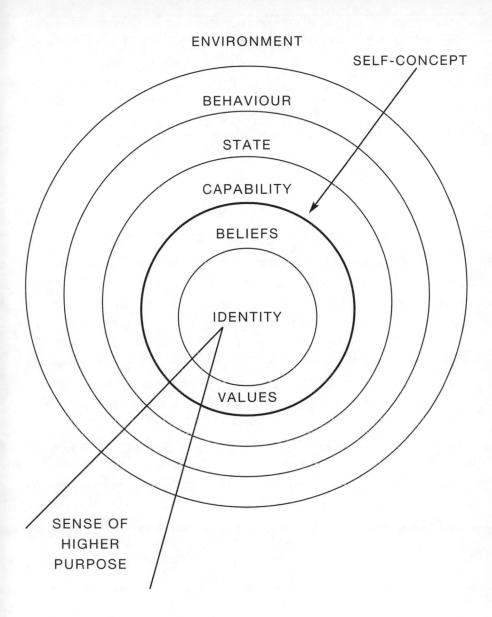

Figure 5.1 A model of the human being

identity so we will place them at the same logical level. The two central areas of the model – the identity and the beliefs/values levels – combine to form the individual's enduring opinion of himself or herself. It is almost as if this self-concept is the engine of the person, in the same way that a vehicle has a source of power.

Carl Rogers,[2] a noted psychotherapist, explored the idea of the self-concept in some depth from the viewpoint of helping individuals make personal changes in their lives. He used such terms as 'ideal self' and 'remembered self' to differentiate between how a person would like to see themselves and how they believed they had actually performed in the past. This is also a contentious area in terms of whether we can define 'self' in specific detail, and what it does is to reinforce the importance of beliefs and perception when we are attempting to make changes in our organisations.

If we return to the analogy of the engine, we can develop this model in more detail. No engine is of use unless it is installed in some sort of vehicle or connected to some sort of system in order to harness its power. Engines need capability for us to realise the potential power they can generate.

No human being can make much in the way of a contribution to society unless they have resources at their disposal including their own knowledge. In human terms, capability is created from a variety of sources: knowledge, money or budgets, personal contacts, technological support and so on. However, simply having a strong identity, positive beliefs, clear values and potential capability is not enough to create excellent behaviour. It is our state, both mental and physical, that determines whether we can access our potential ability. The engine and vehicle analogy is useful here to explain the importance of state.

If we are driving a car with a manual gearbox, we need to ensure that we are in the right gear to transfer the engine power to the driving wheels. A car with a three-litre engine will stall if we try to move off uphill in fifth gear, even though we have a large engine and tremendous performance potential. However, a small car, with a one-litre engine, will perform well if we move off in first gear, on a level road. It is not so much the engine size which matters but how we use the engine power at our disposal. In short, it is the state in which we find ourselves operating that is one of the true determinants of excellent performance. Likewise with a person, if they are not in a positive state, they will not be able to tap into that potential even if they have a powerful 'engine' with a high level of capability such as knowledge, financial resources and energy. This is where stress becomes relevant. A workforce where people are stressed, or where a high degree of 'management by fear' is present will simply not be in a position to add maximum value to the work

of the organisation.

■ Individuals and teams

This model can be used to explain the characteristics of teams as well as of individuals. In fact it can be extended to describe whole organisations and even political systems. However, we change some of the terms when using the approach to describe an organisation. Rather than talk about the state of the organisation, we tend to find it more useful to refer to the idea of the 'culture' or 'climate' – the way things tend to happen in the organisation and 'atmosphere' or 'feel' of the organisation. Although these are not very scientific terms, there is a considerable degree of common understanding about what they mean, and they do seem to help explain why some organisations are good places to be and that some organisations are very unhealthy from a human viewpoint. Leaders create culture and so play a vital role in ensuring that the organisation has the ability to tap into the potential of its workforce. And every workforce has enormous reserves of untapped potential.

We talk in terms of the behaviour level for individuals. If we use the model to describe team or company performance, then it is useful to use operational effectiveness or quality of behaviour to describe the impact on the outside world or environment or, indeed, marketplace.

The state the person is in, or the culture of the team or organisation, determines how they actually behave. And it is this behaviour that actually impacts on the environment. So often we focus on behaviour because it is the aspect of human performance we can most easily assess. This has led to some problems with assessing the impact of training because so often, training seeks to change behaviour without addressing the issues of the beliefs that support that behaviour. A classic example of this challenge is customer care training. It is possible to devote substantial resources to a customer care training programme which seeks to change the behaviours of front-line people and improve the way they deal with customers.

The problem is that, unless the beliefs about the customer are in tune with the new behaviours then, under pressure, the individual will revert to those behaviours which support their true beliefs. For example, although an employee might smile at the customer, use their name correctly and wish them 'have a nice day', if the employee believes deep down that customers are a nuisance, then when a problem arises that belief will come to the fore. All the new behaviours will disappear and the employee will probably become embroiled in an argument or other unproductive transaction with the customer. Beliefs always underlie behaviour which comes naturally. In a change programme, it is no good trying to change behaviour unless we work at changing the underlying beliefs.

Finally, our behaviour impacts on the environment which in turn tends also to shape the behaviour. In a noisy environment we will tend to talk louder – in a tranquil church we will tend to talk quietly. The importance of environment must not be overlooked if we want to create a truly aligned change programme.

If we return to the centre of the diagram in Figure 5.1, one final point is that individuals often feel part of something greater than themselves – a sense of higher purpose often prevails. This may show itself with membership of clubs, and societies or identification with certain causes. Understanding that most people do want to feel part of something is an important part of successful corporate leadership, yet it is one which is often overlooked. People work for a variety of reasons, not just financial reward, and the feeling that you are part of something valuable which is greater than yourself can itself be a powerful source of motivation.

Perhaps the most important point about this diagram is that changes that take place at the centre tend to ripple outwards and invariably affect the outer rings of the diagram. A belief change, for example, will invariably shift a person's state and cause different behaviour. However, changes at the levels of the outer rings do not necessarily produce changes towards the centre of the diagram. For example, changes at the behaviour or environmental level may or may not affect beliefs or the sense of identity.

■ Making changes at the core

The learning point for the leader contemplating change is, of course, to realise that the key to influencing individuals is to operate at the identity, beliefs and values levels, rather than to simply try to change behaviour or create a different environment. In fact truly effective change occurs when all of these levels are aligned which means in organisational terms, the leader needs to pay attention to environment, behaviour, culture, capability, beliefs, values and identity all at the same time. Quite a task!

Leaders, at the top of our organisations, are in a very powerful position to influence behaviour by influencing individuals' beliefs. Very few leaders, certainly in our commercial organisations, seem to acknowledge this fact.

They try to influence performance levels through external or environmental rewards – 'hygiene factors' in Herzberg's terms – without realising that it is the beliefs people have about the organisation and the extent to which they believe they are making a valued contribution which determines behaviour and quality of performance.

Changing Beliefs – a case study

Watts Blake Bearne & Co. PLC is the world's leading international ball clay producer based in the West Country of England in Newton Abbot, a small market town. It has a number of offices and operations worldwide which include locations in the UK, Holland, Portugal, Spain, France, Hong Kong, Germany, Singapore, Indonesia, Thailand, Ukraine, Italy, China and the USA. Each year, the company runs an externally facilitated International Leadership Development Programme designed to develop the leadership skills of young managers in the various parts of the organisation as part of its succession planning process. The Chief Executive, Graham Lawson, along with many other members of the Board and the Senior Management Team within the Company visit the course programme several times to show their commitment and interest in developing their younger managers.

As part of that programme, Graham Lawson gives a talk which he entitles 'Lawson's Rules of Never' (see Table 5.1) designed to promote the course members to think about some basic issues in leadership, in particular the example that they are setting to their work teams.

One organisation that has realised the influence of the leader in shaping both the organisational culture and the beliefs of individuals is Watts Blake Bearne & Company PLC, a ball clay producer based in the West of England. We were so impressed with the attitude of the company to its employees and the issue of succession planning for its leaders of tomorrow that we present it as a mini case study. There are a number of significant issues which occurred to us about this company. Firstly, the top management team are prepared to spend time investing in developing the up-and-coming members of the organisation both in financial terms and in terms of their own personal time. Contact with the senior management on the course programme we describe happens during evening sessions, often until the early hours of the morning. During these sessions, the discussions are very informal and tremendous integration of the company occurs. Course participants come to realise the underlying values and beliefs of their top management team and

Table 5.1 Lawson's Rules of Never

'THE TASK OF THE LEADER IS TO GET HIS OR HER PEOPLE FROM WHERE THEY ARE TO WHERE THEY HAVE NEVER BEEN.' *Henry Kissinger*

In leadership and life always remember these rules:

NEVER

- say something can't be done (Missions Impossible are quite rare!)
- underestimate the power of teamwork (*ordinary people can achieve extraordinary things*)
- accept anything less than excellence, especially of yourself
- be satisfied for longer than an instant
- get complacent (*you never know everything!*)
- walk away from tough decisions (*things only get worse*)
- underestimate competitors (*they are smart people too!*)
- stop listening, questioning and innovating (*there's always a better way*)
- be afraid of taking risks (*except with health and safety issues*)
- waste an opportunity to make an input ('*I didn't think it was my job*')
- underestimate your customers (*your salary depends on them*)
- surprise your boss (*positively is OK, but negatively never!*)
- fail to learn from your mistakes (*all clever people make mistakes; stupidity is making the same mistake twice*)
- fail to give credit to those who deserve it (*let someone else score the goals*)
- forget to say 'thank you' for a job well done (*these two words are the most underused in any language*)

and **ALWAYS**

- tell the truth, no matter how difficult
- keep your promises!

'IF YOU'RE NOT IN BUSINESS FOR FUN OR PROFIT, WHAT THE HELL ARE YOU DOING HERE?' ROBERT TOWNSEND

---

begin to understand that life at the top of an organisation is not always as easy as it might first appear.

Graham Lawson, the Chief Executive, is highly qualified both in scientific and academic terms, yet at the same time retains the common touch with regard to interpersonal and people skills. And it is this appropriate mix of both task and relationship leader behaviour which occurs again and again where we have seen effective change leadership. People will rise to the challenge of change when they are consulted and feel valued. They do not like to be changed by a directive, uncaring management that is only interested in the bottom-line financial figures.

One of the most clearly visible aspects of change at the individual level is the idea of the comfort zone. Human beings seem to be predisposed to working towards what might be called 'negative entropy' (i.e. we all like to work towards order and predictability). Most people seem to agree that the need for structure and order tends to increase as an individual progresses through their life. If we were to plot the ability to cope with change of say a thousand people throughout their lives, we would probably see a trend-line such as that shown in Figure 5.2.

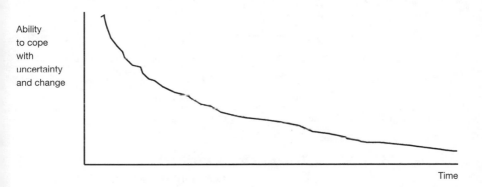

Figure 5.2 The change ability decay curve

The problem is, of course, that as we have already mentioned, the level of change we perceive in the world around us seems to be developing at an ever-increasing rate. We could represent this increase on another graph as shown in Figure 5.3.

When we put these two graphs together, we can see the problem. (Figure 5.4).

There is an obvious predicament that is shown up by these diagrams. During the early part of an individual's life, his or her ability to cope with uncertainty and change often appears to exceed the uncertainty and change to which the individual feels exposed. Thus, young people are often restless

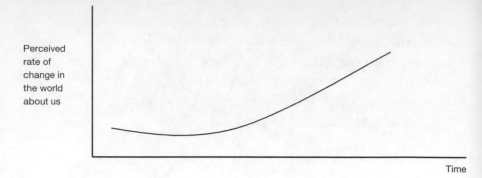

Figure 5.3 The accelerating rate of change

and actually seek stimulation (for example, often through risk-taking activities, drug taking and so on). As the individual matures, then there seems often to be a time or period when the individual's ability to cope with external change, stimulation and uncertainty is well matched with his or her environment. This usually coincides with the peak of the person's career or personal life success. Ultimately, however, a time seems to come for many people when the perceived rate of change and uncertainty exceeds their inherent ability to cope. This may lead to stress, self-doubt and resistance to change as a way of coping with the situation. What the leader needs to realise at this stage is that the harder you push the resistant individual, the harder they tend to push back.

What is needed is a way of dealing with resistant individuals so that they respond positively to change. We want them to become committed to continual improvement processes on the basis that the changes are seen to be beneficial rather than as a threat.

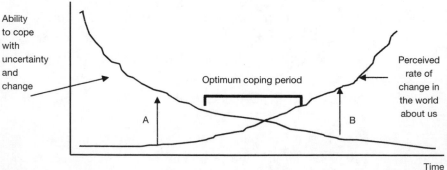

Figure 5.4 The change paradox

It is an interesting aspect of change that people do seem to go through distinct phases in terms of their response to the situation. We have already introduced this idea in Chapter Four. The leader must understand these phases because each needs to be handled in a different way. We will now look at them in more detail.

Initially, an individual will be unaware of the impending change unless they have personally been the initiator. This means that the timing of the first announcement of any major change is critical. The usual problem is that rumours of change tend to leak out in advance giving rise to speculation, false ideas, inaccurate perceptions and so on. The actual management of the announcement phase is key to the whole process of change.

Once the change has been announced, then the reaction of most people is to push the change away, on the basis that it is not necessary or that they do not see the reason for it. As such, they are externalising the change and refusing to believe that it affects them. Thus when we are dealing with change, we are immediately confronting the issue of beliefs, which as we saw in Figure 5.1, tend to be right at the centre of the individual.

Invariably, a major organisational change will have an impact on a person's identity. How do they see themselves coping with the change? Will it devalue the way they see themselves? Does the change clash with the person's values? We can see that change affects the individual fundamentally, and the key to helping individuals respond positively is for the leader to operate at the levels of identity, beliefs and values. Perhaps the most significant avenue to explore is that of self-esteem – the extent to which the individual has a positive image of themselves. So our strategy for making change work at the individual level has to take into account the need for the individual to grow and develop into being confident at handling the new situation.

■ A real case of techno-fear

These phases were highlighted recently with one of our clients, a CEO who was confronted with the need to become computer-literate so that he could work with his other managers on an in-house computer system. The CEO was fifty-three years of age and for several years had steadfastly refused to have a personal computer on his office desk. His argument was that he needed to keep himself divorced from the detail of the business in order to maintain his strategic viewpoint in terms of directing the operation of the company. The reality was, of course, that he was suffering a degree of 'techno-fear' and did not want to expose his lack of knowledge to his colleagues. In fact he was in what we would call the first stage of change perception, the denial phase. When individuals are in the denial phase, they refuse to accept that the change is appropriate and they produce a wide range of arguments as to why the change does not affect them and why they need to take no action. It is very much an external-orientated viewpoint where the person feels they can push the projected change away from them so that they do not become involved.

What invariably happens is that the change does not go away and that the individual often starts to realise that it is 'for real'. When this happens, they tend to internalise the projected change and to begin to feel it does affect them, usually in a negative way. At this stage, they have entered what we might call a 'passive resistance phase' where they do not actually oppose the change, they simply do not make things easy in terms of progressing the issues involved. Eventually, as the change does not go away, they tend to move into the 'active resistance phase' and this is where they may actually sabotage attempts to move things forward.

This active resistance phase showed itself very clearly with the CEO mentioned above. A new Information Technology Manager was appointed to the company and during his first month, the CEO was away from the office on a foreign visit. Unaware of the resistance of the CEO to the computer issue, the new IT Manager arranged for the installation of a new desktop computer on the CEO's desk in his absence. As may be predicted, when he returned, the CEO was not pleased. Although he made a token effort to use the equipment, he succeeded in causing some minor damage, rendering the system useless. He did not do this deliberately but it was almost an unconscious response, which is so often the way the active resistance phase shows itself.

Such resistance phases are the cause of the majority of the problems we encounter in the process of making change work at the individual level. The challenge is how to remove the resistance to then ensure that the person enters the third stage which we will call the exploring stage. With our CEO, the challenge was to break the negative association that he had with the computer. This was achieved by noting that he was a keen golfer and that computer-based golf games are available. Rather than forcing him to use the computer for work right away, the IT Manager concentrated on teaching him how to use the equipment to play the golf game. In doing so, he started the process of building up a positive association about the computer, that is, the equipment represented a pleasurable rather than a threatening experience.

As the CEO developed his confidence, so he started experimenting with the word processor program on the computer. Within a couple of weeks he was typing short memos and starting to access the Management Information System material held on the computer system. Within six months he became very computer-literate and displayed his commitment to the computer system by ensuring that everyone in the company received keyboard skills training, so bringing the company right up to date in electronic terms. In doing so, he had passed from the experimental stage through to the commitment stage, where he once again externalised the change by expressing his commitment publicly and ensuring that others in the company became committed.

The final stage of change adaptation following the commitment stage is what could be called the 'broadcast' stage. This is where the individual becomes so committed to the change that they work hard on converting others to adopt the new ideas. This is where our CEO above ultimately ended up by ensuring that everybody else in the company became computer-literate.

■ The seven phases of human response to change

We can identify seven phases at the individual level:

- **External – non awareness:** 'Blissful ignorance'
- **External – the denial phase:** 'It doesn't affect me . . .'
- **Internal/external – the passive resistance phase:** 'I'll ignore doing anything about this and maybe it'll go away'
- **Internal – the active resistance phase:** 'How can I oppose this threat . . .'
- **Internal – the exploration phase:** 'I'll try but it's risky . . .'
- **External – the commitment phase:** 'This is great, I'm really enjoying this . . .'
- **External – the broadcast phase:** 'Let me tell you about this great idea we've adopted . . .'

The lesson for the leader is that people do need to pass through these phases.

We have already talked about the announcement stage of a change or change programme. Timing and communication channels are vitally important issues in terms of when to announce a change.

With regard to the denial phase, this is probably best handled by giving facts and information together with examples of what other organisations are doing. The idea is to confront the individual with a sound argument so that they cannot simply push the idea of the change away into the distance.

In terms of the resistance phases, then effective communication, particularly listening, becomes important. What we want the individual to do is to articulate their objections and voice them, rather than sweep them under the carpet. Instead of pushing people towards the change which only tends to increase the resistance, it is often better to identify the factors leading in the right direction and those which are holding the individual back. We will look at this idea later in this chapter when we consider Force Field Analysis. By identifying those resistance factors which are holding the individual back and removing them, it is then possible to move into the exploration phase.

What is vital in the exploration phase is that the individual's self-confidence is developed through experiencing 'small chunks of success'. The key to this phase is setting easily achievable goals and targets so that an increasingly positive association is developed. Eventually, enough building blocks of small successes will combine to create a 'critical mass' of positive association with the new order of things and this is where commitment will usually become apparent. Once the individual is committed, then they could and should be encouraged to broadcast that commitment, and so convert other individuals who are less advanced in terms of their position on the 'change phases time-line'.

■ Dealing with change at the individual level

So how can we deal with change more effectively at the individual level? The first thing is to use the ideas of the change phases time-line above to give individuals time to become both adjusted and committed to the new situation.

The second idea is to use Force Field Analysis, as we have already mentioned. Figure 5.5 shows the basic concept. The first step is to describe the present situation in terms of characteristics both desirable and undesirable. In practical terms a traditional SWOT analysis using strengths, weaknesses, opportunities and threats is often the most useful way of tackling this stage.

The second stage is to indulge in some 'blue sky' visioning to create a picture of the future position we want to reach. In this case, the characteristics are usually less concrete than for the present position but they do provide a sense of direction.

The third stage is to consider all the current issues which are tending to push the organisation in the direction of the desired future position – we call these the 'driving forces' – and all the current issues which are holding us back. We call these the 'restraining forces'.

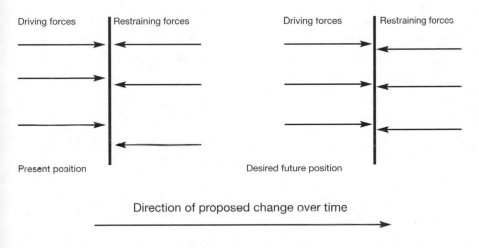

Figure 5.5 Force Field Analysis

What most organisations seem to do is to focus on applying pressure and stepping up the driving forces. The problem with this approach is that it tends to set up resistance, both passive and active, which in turn tends to increase the restraining forces. The net result is that the organisation stays stuck with everyone under more pressure!

The key, of course, is to focus on the restraining forces to try to remove or reduce one or more of them. In this way, the natural pressure of the driving forces will then tend to move things in the right direction. It is at this stage that the driving forces may then be increased, promoting a more rapid advance towards the desired new position.

Eventually the position will settle into a new state of balance with altered **117** driving and restraining forces, but this time in the desired future position as intended. Force Field Analysis is a very useful technique, particularly when we realise that many of the restraining forces are human in nature rather than purely physical. Effective change leadership invariably involves helping people to change their negative beliefs which quite frequently are the source of most of the restraining forces.

Techniques such as Force Field Analysis are useful in that they can lay the problem out in graphical terms in front of the interested parties. As such these techniques become part of the communication process generally. Communication is the key to effective change leadership. It is vital to explain what is happening and make sufficient time for discussion.

Another important aspect of effective change leadership is to invest time and other resources in building the team. Developing a social side can be a very important way of promoting change acceptance, particularly once relationships become deepened and a sense of trust starts to develop. There are two important aspects to team development in this context. Firstly, there is the opportunity to set effective goals both individually and with the team as a whole. Secondly, a common, agreed set of values can be identified and then used as the basis for both discussion and day-to-day operation.

■ Change and stress

Whether individuals are operating on their own or as part of a team, one issue which is important is that change can lead to stress, particularly if the amount of change at any one time exceeds an individual's ability to cope. This is not a new phenomenon. In the 1960s, Holmes and Rahe, two American doctors, investigated the link between change, both positive and negative, and the incidence of serious illness suffered by their group of research subjects. They produced the Social Readjustment Scale which ranked specific life events with the negative impact they tended to have on an individual's health. A modified version of the scale is shown as Table 5.2. It must be stressed that there are many cultural differences between how individuals in different countries react to life events. In some countries, such as the USA, people tend to be more mobile than in some of the European countries, and so Americans may well be less affected by a change in their home residence than, say, a German who has been living in the same town for thirty or more years.

Table 5.2 The life event survey based on the work of Holmes and Rahe

There are many factors which tend to predispose individuals to becoming stressed. In particular the amount of change that has taken place in a particular person's life seems to be important. How much change has there been in your life in the past two years?

Rank	Tick if occurred	Life event	Number of occurrences	Mean Value
1.		Death of a spouse		100
2.		Divorce		73
3.		Marital separation		65
4.		Jail term		63
5.		Death of a close family member		63
6.		Personal injury or illness		53
7.		Marriage		50
8.		Fired at work		47
9.		Marital reconciliation		47
10.		Retirement		45
11.		Change in health of a family member		45
12.		Pregnancy (score applies for both spouses)		44
13.		Sexual difficulties		39
14.		Gain of a new family member		39
15.		Business readjustment		39
16.		Change in financial state		38
17.		Death of a close friend		37
18.		Change to a different line of work		36
19.		Change in number of arguments with spouse		35
20.		Mortgage over £50,000		31
21.		Foreclosure of mortgage or loan		30
22.		Change in responsibilities at work		29
23.		Son or daughter leaving home		29
24.		Trouble with in-laws		29
25.		Outstanding personal achievement		28
26.		Spouse began or stopped work		26
27.		Began or ended schooling		26
28.		Change in living conditions		25
29.		Revision of personal habits		24
30.		Trouble with boss		23
31.		Change in work hours or conditions		20
32.		Change in residence		20
33.		Change in schools		20
34.		Change in recreation		19
35.		Change in church activities		19
36.		Change in social activities		18
37.		Mortgage or loan less than £50,000		17
38.		Change in sleeping		16
39.		Change in number of family get-togethers		15
40.		Change in eating habits		15
41.		Vacation		13
42.		Christmas		12
43.		Minor violations of the law 19		11

Your total score is ....

The Social Readjustment Scale is thus simply a way of comparing typical relative impacts of various life events so that individually we can make an assessment of the extent to which we are asking ourselves to cope with either too much or not enough change. It is also important because of the change adaptation curve, to realise that a person's age can determine the extent to which a given life event is stressful or not. Usually, someone in their early twenties will thrive on moving their home several times in a few years whereas someone in their late sixties might see such a situation as very threatening. Thus, using a specific number of points on the version of the Social Readjustment Scale shown must be taken as a general guideline only. We have taken the liberty of updating some of the figures on the scale and translating them into UK currency. However, the principle of the questionnaire is still the same as in the original study and we have found it a useful way of initiating discussions on the role played by poorly led change in the creation of excessive stress in the workplace.

To complete the scale, tick any life event that has occurred to you during the past two years. For some of the items such as number 13, it may be more appropriate to take into account a change in pattern rather than every specific instance! However, such events as 'dismissed from work' or 'death of a close family member' should be logged as multiple events if more than one occurrence has taken place in the preceding two years. To find your score, read all forty-three statements, tick those which apply to you and log the number of occurrences. For multiple occurrences, multiply the score by the number of times the event has occurred. Then total your score and fill in the space at the bottom of the questionnaire.

Scores greater than 300 tend to suggest that you are experiencing a significant amount of change, and this might lead to your experiencing some stress-related problems. If this is likely, then it might be worth delaying some optional changes to give yourself time to adjust. At the same time, some basic attention to stress management would be advised, such as more exercise, more relaxation and attention to diet.

However, it is not just the higher scores which are significant. Scores of less than 150 can mean that a person is under-stimulated and this can lead to another type of stress reaction called 'rustout' which can be as stressful as too much stimulation. It seems we all need a certain amount of change but not too much!

The learning point for the leader is to become aware of the amount of change he or she is expecting their people to cope with on a day-to-day basis.

For instance, they should plan change as a rolling programme together with building in some stress resilience issues such as promoting out-of-hours social activity, healthy eating, exercise and relaxation. Subsidised sub-scriptions to health clubs can provide a very convenient way of helping people maintain their health and fitness during difficult times of change.

It is obvious that change can have significant impact on individuals and that different individuals have differing levels of resilience to change in terms of how they cope.

A key question to ask is 'how can we increase resilience?' One person, a psychologist in the USA called Price Pritchett, has made a detailed study of developing change resilience and he has produced an excellent series of books, some co-authored with his partner Ron Pound. Prichett and Pound have identified a number of ways in which we need to encourage our colleagues to accept that change is a challenge which is here to stay. We have consolidated and summarised some of their key ideas and combined them with some of our own in Table 5.3.

Fifteen ways are listed in which people can help themselves cope with and avoid stress from change. We present these as some specific ways leaders and managers can help individuals who are struggling to cope with change, as a fundamental part of change leadership should be to help people come to terms with new ways of doing things using some or all of these strategies.

Table 5.3 What do people actually need to DO to cope with change?

1   They need to take personal responsibility for their own life rather than expecting someone else to sort out their stress problems for them.

2. It is important to accept fate, move on and avoid allowing oneself to feel and act like a victim.

3. Pressure in the workplace is here to stay. The best way to cope is to become focused on some specific goals.

4. As change is here to stay, it is important to align yourself to the future vision rather than resisting change.

5. It is important to become familiar with the new rules of the game. How has the game changed?

6. It is important to identify which things you can control and which things are outside your control.

7. In terms of the pace of change, it is important to keep in step with what's happening around you rather than attempting to set your own pace.

8. In the future it is added value which will determine who stays in a job and who goes. Concentrating on how you can re-engineer your job to add extra value is key to future organisational survival.

9. Everything needs to speed up including personal productivity.

10. Instead of fearing the future, control your thoughts, stop worrying and set some goals.

11. Pick battles big enough to matter, small enough to win rather than trying to fight the wrong battles.

12. Get passionate and fall in love with your job.

13. Keep updating your skills and take on new challenges.

14. Develop your tolerance for change and stop trying to eliminate uncertainty.

15. As an employee or manager, don't assume that 'caring management' should make you feel comfortable – do what works.

Effective change leadership is largely about working at the individual level whilst ensuring that we are bringing our strategic vision into operation. It is important that a corporate culture accepts and thrives on change. Also, we need to have powerful advocacy for change in terms of internal change agents, external stakeholders, middle managers and outsiders.

This all requires effective communication and change tactics. The key, however, is to create effective 'champions of change' within the business and recent research by McKinsey and Co. proposes that real change is actually driven from the middle of the organisation as well as from the top. The McKinsey team – Jon Katzenbach and his colleagues – have suggested the characteristics of 'real change leaders',[3] that is, those managers in the middle of the organisation that ensure new initiatives are successful (see Table 5.4).

Table 5.4 The characteristics of real change leaders

- Commitment to a better way
- Courage to challenge the existing power bases and norms
- Personal initiative to go beyond defined boundaries
- Motivation of themselves and others
- Caring about how people are treated and enabled to perform
- Staying undercover and not seeking glory
- Maintaining a sense of humour about themselves and their situations

■ Summary

In this chapter we have explored the impact of change on the individual. We have looked at a model to explain why individuals tend to resist change and how we can help people to work through the phases of change adaptation. If we carry this out effectively, then we will avoid many of the stress problems associated with change and create a critical mass of individuals who will, in turn, move the organisation forward in both operational and front-line terms by turning the strategic vision into reality.

At the individual level, the key skill of the leader is in creating a climate where change is welcomed, not feared. Human beings need the stimulation of change in order to grow and develop. Invariably it is in the presentation of the case for change that the problems occur. As Shakespeare once said, 'there is nothing either good or bad, but thinking makes it so.'

The real test of effective change leadership is in the selling of the change, creating emotional alignment, and winning hearts and minds. That is the subject of our next chapter.

Endnotes

1   Joseph O'Connor and John Seymour (1990), Introducing NLP, Mandala
2   Carl Rogers (1967), On Becoming a Person, Constable
3   Jon Katzenbach et al. (1996), Real Change Leaders, Nicholas Brealey

Appetiser

CHAPTER SIX

In this chapter, you will:

■ FIND OUT ABOUT THE LEADERSHIP CRISIS WE ALL FACE

■ DISCOVER THE DIFFERENCE BETWEEN EXCELLENT RESULTS AND AVERAGE RESULTS IN CHANGE LEADERSHIP

■ IDENTIFY THE IMPORTANCE OF HOW LEADERS ACTUALLY BEHAVE IN 'WALKING THE TALK'

■ BE REMINDED THAT IN ORDER FOR THE LEADER TO WIN THE 'HEARTS AND MINDS' OF THE PEOPLE, IT IS VITAL TO COMMUNICATE THE REASONS FOR CHANGE AND THUS CREATE UNDERSTANDING

■ COME TO REALISE THAT IT IS UNCERTAINTY THAT IS THE MAIN CAUSE OF ANXIETY IN CHANGE PROGRAMMES

■ REALISE THAT ORGANISATIONAL LEADERS MUST TARGET THE ELIMINATION OF NEGATIVE COMPANY POLITICS THROUGH OPEN COMMUNICATION

■ REDISCOVER THE IMPORTANCE OF INTEGRITY IN LEADERSHIP

■ LEARN THE KEY ATTRIBUTES OF EFFECTIVE CHANGE LEADERSHIP IN WINNING HEARTS AND MINDS.

The 'Hearts and Minds' of Leadership

'British business has a leadership crisis – we have failed to distinguish between management skills and qualities of leadership.' This statement appeared in the *Daily Telegraph* in December 1998. It followed on from an Institute of Directors survey[1] earlier that year which revealed that Leadership and Strategic Development were the two most relevant boardroom issues. That year also produced some spectacular leadership casualties including Martin Taylor (Barclays Bank), Dick Brown (Cable & Wireless), and others at Rank, United Utilities, BAA and EMI. The experience in UK was also being reflected elsewhere in the world, particularly in the business and banking sectors in Japan.

However, by far the biggest leadership failure of 1998 and 1999 was the ongoing saga of Bill Clinton's Presidency. The constant examination of his moral standing and credibility as a result of the Monica Lewinsky affair virtually paralysed Washington for the whole of that period, and this damaged the USA's reputation; there was a hollow ring to the title of 'world leader'. Interestingly, this paralysis contributed to the extraordinary rise to prominence of UK Prime Minister Tony Blair on to the world stage, primarily through his leadership role in the NATO war against Serbia in 1999.

This apart, the worrying number of leadership 'failures' at the end of the twentieth century raises some fundamental questions about the relationship between those charged with leading their organisations and their constituents. Has the last period of the millennium been a particularly difficult one for the leaders at the top of organisations – or was this just a continuation of the issues which have always faced other individuals in similar situations throughout history? Why have people, with a high reputation and recruited in good faith, failed to deliver? Is there a mismatch between expectation and delivery? Is there an inherent difficulty when a 'new' leader tries to change an 'old' culture? Have the pressures of leading in continuous change become too great?

These, and other issues, will be addressed in this chapter, in the context of the relationship between the 'leader' and the 'team'. In constant change, the key to effective leadership is the ability to motivate and get the best out of people. This is nothing new; winning hearts and minds has always been important. However, the speed of change that we are now experiencing, continually changing technology and the ever-increasing complexities of life, all combine to make this relationship especially difficult. People in leadership roles are finding this difficult – even those with considerable experience. We need to discover the heart of the problem, and then to address the relevant issues in order to come up with practical guidelines for 'tomorrow's leaders'. Recruiting chief executives who subsequently fail, for whatever reason, is a costly exercise with severe implications for both the individual and the organisation. The purpose of this chapter is to help towards a better understanding of this vital topic, so that there are fewer casualties in the future.

■ Voyage of discovery

In the research for this book, we were struck by the fact that there were many people at the top of organisations, in both the private and the public sectors, who appeared to be leading their organisations through change particularly successfully. Although some of these individuals were well-known, others were not, even if their companies were. At first sight, this appeared to be rather strange. After all, during the 1980s and early 1990s the public were familiar with names such as John Harvey-Jones, Tiny Rowlands, Lord Hanson, Jack Welch and Lord Weinstock. And yet, whenever we asked at our seminars for people to name current top business leaders, the only two that were consistently mentioned were Richard Branson and Bill Gates.

As a result, we have interviewed some twenty-five top leaders in an attempt to discover what it is that they are doing so effectively to motivate their people to achieve really good results. During this voyage of discovery, we learned a number of important points. First, although some were achieving 'outstanding' results, others had only managed 'very good'. It soon became evident that this was immaterial since, on a journey of continuous change, it is not possible to manage to produce excellent results all the time.

By definition, 'excellent results' are not the norm. The environment is constantly altering and as organisations adjust accordingly, so their learning experience has to adjust as well. One has only to look at the Marks & Spencer example, as they struggled to recover lost ground under Peter Salisbury's new leadership in 1999, to realise how quickly a company whose name had been associated with excellence for so long can find itself struggling, with little warning.

Second, there were certain behaviours that these individuals had which provided a constancy which sustained them through both good times and bad. These will now be discussed in detail and are identified under the following titles: creating understanding; effective communications; releasing potential; personal example; and self-pacing.

Creating understanding

'One of the most difficult aspects of leadership is getting people to consider the reason for change.'[2] This comment by John Roberts (Chief Executive, The Post Office) underlines the problem of creating understanding throughout an organisation which is involved in continual change. One of the really difficult issues for leaders is to turn the vision into reality. As Sir Paul Condon (the Commissioner of the Metropolitan Police Service) put it: 'It is the difficulty of the disconnection between a policy statement and implementation.'[3]

This creation of understanding is not just difficult for the followers – it is also testing for the leaders. An environment of continual change means that those operating at board level are often struggling with highly complex issues with only a limited time to analyse all the relevant factors. We can therefore have a situation where senior management is having a difficulty with understanding the issues themselves and, as a consequence, they are not in a position to provide clear thinking for the rest of the organisation. This lack of clarity can lead to frustration through a failure of communication between senior executives and the organisation. The key to this problem is a communication system which enables constant updating, briefing and feedback so that everyone is aware of the size of the issue, what is in the minds of the senior team, and how this thinking will impact on to everybody's area of responsibility. We have already seen in Chapter Four how the communications system at Honda assisted this process. 'Creating understanding at all levels is difficult, which is why we have developed this system' (Ken Keir, Managing Director, Honda UK).[4]

This creation of understanding is made more difficult for two reasons: fear of uncertainty; and a paucity of intellectual capability throughout organisations.

The fear of uncertainty is a natural human instinct that affects all of us from time to time. Whether we are the type of person who is excited by change or not, most of us are comfortable in an environment which we understand, and are able to perform effectively. We also tend to be happiest in such circumstances. Even those who thrive on change appreciate a period of stability occasionally. It is therefore hardly surprising that uncertainty can destabilise most people, which, in turn, affects their happiness and therefore their ability to perform well. Unless this issue is addressed properly, it can spread like a cancer throughout an organisation.

It is the role of leaders (at every level) to tackle 'uncertainty' systematically by pursuing a policy of open communication, using every opportunity to discuss and explain all the relevant aspects of the change process. This should involve a good deal of listening, and the readiness to change original ideas as a result of consultation. The most effective counter to the fear of change is 'ownership'. This enables everybody to become involved in the process and to feel that they have a proper part to play in the development of ideas and, as a result, the progression of the company. This early removal of uncertainty, through ownership, is a most effective leadership process.

The second issue is a much more fundamental problem. There appears to be a paucity of intellectual capability on the part of many leaders in significant leadership roles in many of our organisations. In his usual succinct way, Warren Bennis put his finger on the heart of the problem when he said: 'In a knowledge workers' society, we will need leaders at every level who are extraordinarily brainy.'[5] He went on to explain in his interview with *People Management* that in order to deal with complex issues, we needed to rethink how to educate people for business.

However, it goes much further than that – and the implications are fundamental. It is not just business which needs this reappraisal, it affects every organisation in both the public and private sectors, throughout the developed world. The extraordinary technological developments, epitomised by the Internet, which give us far more choices than even a couple of years ago, has exposed a widening gap between those who have the intellectual capacity to cope with these exciting advancements, and those who do not.

Unless we re-educate people throughout organisations and develop their cognitive skills, companies will not be able to manage the challenges of the future. Indeed, this is already beginning to happen, exemplified by one of the new UK banks who admitted to us that unless they addressed this issue they doubted whether they would be able to cope with the complexities of the future which, in turn, could affect their ability to remain as a retail bank.

There is a realisation that national educational systems are not adjusting sufficiently quickly to the changing nature of the work environment. This is particularly acute in the UK where, at the higher level, the expansion of universities in the 1990s hid this failure and, at the school level, there is a very worrying low standard of education. Warren Bennis has already drawn attention to a similar problem in the USA, and the situation is reflected, to a greater or lesser extent, in other countries throughout the world.

Whilst the education issue is beyond the scope of this book, the implications for leadership and 'creating understanding' are nonetheless clear. Unless we are able to raise substantially the intellectual capability of people throughout organisations, it will be extremely difficult for leaders to bring about effective change in the future. People need to be able to really understand the reasons for change.

Effective communications

Part of the process of creating understanding is effective communications. It is particularly difficult when managing change because, as we have already seen, leaders are often struggling to clarify their own thinking as well as trying to communicate a clear message throughout the organisation at the same time. Unless there is a clarity of thought, there is a danger that leaders will give a mixed message, which can lead to confusion.

We therefore need to understand what is really required from those in leadership roles in order for them to achieve effective communication. The important first step is to have a clear strategy right from the outset. This is particularly important when an individual first assumes a new appointment. As John Roberts pointed out in his discussion with us, 'It was important for me to start with a clear agenda when I took over as Chief Executive of the Post Office. In retrospect, I wish my agenda had been clearer at the beginning.'[6] The problem is that an individual has so much to absorb when taking over a new job, that it is difficult to be clear about priorities, let alone about strategy. As if this is not enough, they will also be pressurised by their team to communicate their ideas. In such circumstances it is very tempting to take decisions and issue instructions too early.

In facing such a situation when assuming a new appointment as CEO, one of the authors resisted all calls to communicate his ideas for the first month. He used this period to get to know the organisation, and to listen. When his induction was over – and when he was ready – he then communicated his thoughts to everybody by means of a series of verbal briefings.

Although it may not be possible to delay initial communication for as long as this, it is crucially important that the first message from a new leader has been thought through carefully. It is also important that the means of communication which are used by the organisation are utilised properly. These will vary, depending on the culture of the company; however, following the 'normal' system is especially relevant because it indicates that the new incumbent is sensitive to the culture. This is an important ritual because it indicates the leader's willingness to adapt which, in turn, will encourage the employees to listen with an open mind. It also reinforces the position of those operating at middle-management level.

Once the general way forward is clear, it is essential that the senior management team maintain open communications with every individual in that group. This is especially difficult in change due to complexity, speed, volume of work and various other associated factors. It requires a real effort to ensure that everybody is kept in the picture. Once again, and on the assumption that the current practice is effective, it is advisable to stick to the normal procedures. The important thing is to ensure that they contain an automatic system which ensures good communication. Examples of effective procedures include those used by the military (fully tested in conditions of war) and the 'circles' management system adopted by Honda. It is also important that the open system used at senior level is reflected right throughout the organisation. The ability for every individual to challenge ideas and query points of detail is essential in order to develop confidence in the trust and the integrity of the organisation (all the chief executives to whom we spoke stressed the importance of this point).

The purpose of such a systematic approach to open communications is to break down the barriers to the change process that will be erected from some quarters. These barriers will only be removed through the energetic enthusiasm of leaders at all levels. This can be very wearing and will require considerable persistence, particularly because it is likely to involve office politics – either because someone is trying to undermine the message or, more likely, because politics is endemic within the company. This is a common scenario which can test the patience of most leaders, assuming that they are not involved with political intrigue themselves! The behaviour of the boss in these circumstances is crucial. Gail Rebuck (Chief Executive, Random House Group) made the position quite clear: 'I'm allergic to company politics! I meet conflict head on and bring it out into the open to resolve it. This seems to work because people know that I will not play politics. It's such a waste of time.'[7]

Having 'set the direction and ensured that it is translated internally' (John Roberts), the final part of the process is persistence. Tim Melville-Ross (Director General, Institute of Directors) stressed the importance of this behaviour: 'In order to ensure effective change it is important to give a persistent message the whole time.'[8] This requires planning, energy and patience. Planning, in that the leader needs to clarify their thoughts in advance; energy, in that the leader will need to give the same message again and again to everybody they meet, both formally and informally – over a long period; and patience, because they will be required to answer numerous questions.

Of all the points raised in this section, this latter one is probably the most important. It is the behaviour of the leader which will have the greatest impact, and its importance is based on the fact that only by spending time and energy in meeting people and explaining the message will the genuine concerns of people be addressed. 'In order for people to change, they have to be convinced of the reasons for change'[9] (Jim Mowatt, National Secretary, Transport & General Workers Union). In order to be really effective, however, this behaviour of 'the leader' needs to be reflected by the rest of the management team.

Releasing potential

Perhaps the key to achieving effective change leadership is to enable the release of all of people's potential within the organisation. In most companies this potential lies dormant, and will remain so unless something is done to change the status quo. It is similar to an iceberg with 70% hidden below the surface (see Figure 6.1). This is not only a leadership challenge, it is also a means to help the leader. We will address this latter issue later on in the chapter but, for now, we will concentrate on how to release potential.

The first point to make is that this is probably the most rewarding and exciting thing that a leader can achieve. All the chief executives to whom we spoke referred to the sense of pride in seeing their people achieve their

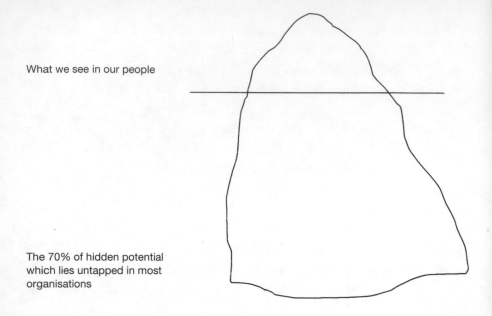

What we see in our people

The 70% of hidden potential
which lies untapped in most
organisations

Figure 6.1 The iceberg principle of human potential

potential. Mair Barnes (the first woman to be Managing Director of Woolworths) said, 'I believe passionately in developing people. If you can remove the barriers and the limiting perceptions then everyone can grow, provided you nurture them. Releasing that energy and encouraging people to flower is magical.'[10]

Ken Keir linked it to the creation of understanding and said: 'The most rewarding aspect of leading an organisation through change is seeing the comprehension of understanding by everyone involved in the process.'[11] Not only is it most rewarding, it could be argued that releasing potential of individuals is one of the fundamental aspects of leadership. In order to manage this really effectively it requires the leader to, quite literally, excite people to achieve their optimum.

It is generally acknowledged that 'ownership' is a key ingredient to effecting change. However, 'ownership really has to mean something' (Sir Stuart Hampson, Chairman, John Lewis Partnership).[12] This is achieved in the John Lewis Partnership in two ways. Firstly, all the employees or 'Partners' receive a share of the profits at the end of each financial year. Secondly, Hampson goes to exceptional lengths to create a climate in the company where Partners are trusted with the kind of confidential information which most businesses restrict to a few individuals at the top. Hampson believes that employees perform more effectively and with a greater sense of ownership if they know the full picture.

There are other companies doing the same, perhaps the best example in UK being Asda. It is an excellent means of motivation and helps to encourage everybody to get involved in the process. However, money does not have to be the only form of motivation, indeed, studies would lead us to believe that it is less important than is generally thought. Ownership embraces anything that enables people to feel that their contribution is both worthwhile and valued.

A good example of this, which also involves creativity, became apparent when one of the authors visited RAF Cosford in 1998. The purpose of the station is to train technicians for the RAF front line. One of the difficulties which the instructors were encountering was to explain the hydraulic system effectively, so that the students could really understand the process. One of the instructors solved the problem by producing a short video which demonstrated the process by means of impressive graphics. He achieved this in a matter of weeks, having never made a video before and without any training on computer graphics. The film was of high quality which would not have looked out of place as part of a BBC documentary. In addition, the students' understanding was helped significantly, the instructor took great pride in his achievement and, best of all, his officers celebrated his innovative idea. It was seen as a real team effort – and an example of 'released' potential brought about by obvious encouragement for a valued contribution.

In an environment of continual change, leaders need to champion innovation and creativity. Unless they achieve this, organisations will be unable to keep up with the pace of change in the future. The problem is that, unlike in the RAF, many of today's senior managers do not have the confidence to empower their people properly, let alone the imagination to encourage individuals with flair. In an environment of exciting technological change that will be the norm in future, it would seem imperative that the leaders of tomorrow acquire the necessary skill to support individuals to develop their creativity to the full.

Personal example

Personal example is a fundamental aspect of leadership and nowhere is this more vital than during the process of managing change. The way leaders behave, the manner in which they treat people, their attitude to ethical matters, and their reaction in periods of difficulty are all observed by their followers. The subsequent commitment to change will depend fundamentally on the judgement of that observation. The key point here is that nobody knows better about the behaviour of a leader than their followers. If they are not convinced, they will not follow.

In answer to the question 'what is important in the way you do business?' all the chief executives to whom the authors spoke said: 'Integrity.' Integrity, honesty and trust are such simple words, but their implications for leadership are enormous. They provide the glue which binds leaders and followers together. However, unlike quick-setting adhesive, it takes a long time to establish this bond as both sides test out their relationship and gradually establish a pattern of working together. It is grounded in transparency, and the relationship will be tested time and time again before both sides are satisfied that it works.

Nobody pretends that this is easy, especially in a change process where, for instance, senior management may not be able to be entirely open due to the sensitivity of issues which they are still debating at strategic level. Such a situation underlines the real dilemma, which is that it is not possible to be 'half-open'; there is either a fully open atmosphere, or there is not. It is therefore crucial that difficult aspects of relationships are tackled immediately so that no mistrust is allowed to fester. For, although it takes a long time to establish trust, it can be broken in a minute. Once that has occurred, it may never be rebuilt – as a number of teams can testify.

One of the most effective ways of building trust is for the leader to share the working experience of followers. This can take many forms but, fundamentally, it involves managers getting out of their offices and dis- covering what life is really like at the coalface. Most of the chief executives to whom we spoke spend a significant time away from their offices, meeting people. For instance, Ken Keir spends three and a half days a week away, Jim Mowatt is known for visiting his members on their night-shifts and the Retail Director of Woolworths, Leo McKee visits around 200 stores per year.[13]

Not only does such behaviour signal that the leader is really interested in their people, it also provides the opportunity for employees to voice their concerns, and to raise issues in an informal atmosphere. Provided that the leader listens and responds in an open and honest manner, trust will be established which, in most cases, will hold firm in periods of difficulty. It is therefore important that the leader establishes a pattern of such visits right from the start, so that the bond is 'set' before any crisis arises.

All that we have discussed so far in this chapter could equally be applied to the management of the *status quo*. However, in order to lead an organisation through continuous change, something extra is required – leaders need to 'champion' change. This involves an enthusiasm for change, reinforced with energy and passion. Unless there is enthusiastic leadership one cannot expect the organisation to embrace change fully. The energy required should not be underestimated, particularly over a long period, and it is an issue which we will discuss in the next section. Passion is needed because without this it will not be possible to sustain leadership for very long.

Of these three, probably passion is the key, since managing change today requires enormous resilience and, without passion, it is difficult to see how an individual can sustain themselves over a long period. We need to be quite clear about this – there is no place any longer for those focused on short-term gain in a world of perpetual change. The simple comment by Gail Rebuck that she has a passion for books underpins her determination to achieve excellence with Random House.

The example required of leaders can best be summarised by the three 'Ps' – Passion, Praise and Pride. A passion for change; praise for people's efforts; and pride in the results of the team.

Self-pacing

The last of the behaviours exemplified by the leaders to whom we spoke is 'self-pacing.' All of us are finding it increasingly difficult to cope with the speed of change, it is therefore hardly surprising that those at the top of organisations are finding it exhausting. When asked what she found difficult to do, Gail Rebuck replied: 'Having the energy to cope with the pace of change.'[14] In an article in *The Times Magazine* in 1994, Martin Taylor (then Chief Executive of Barclays Bank) remarked that it was necessary to be young at the top. 'I don't think I could do this job the way I'm trying to do it if I were five years older. Certainly at the beginning of this year, I was absolutely at the limits of my stamina, which is reasonably high.'[15] Amongst other aspects, the article drew attention to the fact that, in the mid-1990s, men in their early forties were being sought to run organisations because of their energy (it included profiles of three leaders aged between forty-one and forty-three: Martin Taylor, Tony Blair and Howard Davies, then Director-General of the CBI). Such is the increasing pressures at the top that, four years later, Steven

Cain was appointed as Chief Executive of Carlton Communications at the age of thirty-four.

We have already seen the average age of CEOs on appointment drop from early fifties to early forties within a decade, and it will be interesting to see whether this downward trend is continued in the future. Whether it is or not, the enormous pressures on people operating at the top of organisations has resulted in a number of casualties, including Martin Taylor. Therefore the requirement for leaders to pace themselves is fundamental.

This 'self-pacing' can be developed, just like any other skill. Our sample Chief Executives were particularly good at managing their time and it was most noticeable that all of them had a routine for coping with their enormous time pressures: John Roberts 'spent time managing time'; Sir Paul Condon managed time 'ruthlessly'; Ken Keir had a good PA; and Gail Rebuck was good at saying 'no'. What all of them had realised, from early on in their careers, was the essential importance of living a disciplined life as a means of controlling the pressures of time. This essential discipline is more important for leaders today there it has ever been. So much so that, unless an individual is able to exercise effective self-discipline over time-management, they are unlikely to be able to cope with the increasing pace of change.

Linked with time-management is the requirement to maintain a balance in one's life. Once again, our Chief Executives were good at this and made a point of managing the 'home–work' conflict. Melville-Ross and Roberts guarded their weekends jealously; Rebuck ensured that she got home by 8pm a couple of nights during the week, in order to see the children; and to Condon, leave is sacrosanct. All of them were quite clear about the importance of this balance. It gave them the opportunity to maintain energy levels over a lengthy period, as well as giving their brain a rest from the relentless demands of their jobs.

It is important for those in leadership roles, at any level, to ensure that they maintain a balanced life and thus prevent their work becoming too oppressive. This can be achieved in many ways (such as interests in sport, hobbies, leisure activities or the family), and each individual will have their own preferences; the important thing is to actively develop such interests, and not to become a slave to the job. Not only is this bad for one's health, it can also result in one becoming a boring leader!

The third aspect of 'self-pacing' is that of delegation. Tim Melville-Ross admitted that when he first took over as Chief Executive of Nationwide he tried to do too much himself. As a result, he found himself doing too much work, whilst those around him became frustrated because they were not doing enough, consequently the senior management was not operating effectively. His admission reflects the experience of countless CEOs on first taking up their appointments, and it requires individuals to take positive steps to counter this common failing. This becomes even more prevalent during change, especially as leaders can be tempted to respond to increasing workload by doing it all themselves, rather than distributing appropriate jobs to those who are more capable.

So far we have concerned ourselves with the requirement of the leader to pace themselves, but this is equally important for the organisation, and it is therefore an outcome of leadership. Good leaders are sensitive to the impact of the change process on their people and adjust the pace of change accordingly. They are aware of the need to encourage ownership through dialogue and empowerment, they are alert to the importance of frequent reviews (in order to assess the impact of the speed of the changes being implemented), and also the requirement to achieve alterations by small steps.

Good leaders adopt a flexibility to the pace of change, matching it to the capability of their people so that, ideally, they are able to take everything in their stride. This takes time – much longer than you think. As Mair Barnes[16] observed: 'It is important not to falter on the way. It takes much longer than you expect – and you have to go much deeper than you think.' She also talked about the need to 'bore down' selectively, a point that was also noted by Sir Peter Davis: 'You have to bore down below the mezzanine layer to find out what is actually happening – and that takes time.'[17]

This skill (for it is a skill) of flexibility is the mark of a proficient leader. It requires hard work, sensitivity and, quite often, the requirement for the leader to admit that they have got the 'self-pacing' wrong. However, this ability, which is so often learnt through bitter experience, is very important because it can be the key to operating at optimum level over an extended period. In a world of continuous change this is most relevant.

It is hardly surprising that, in our survey, those Chief Executives who were self-disciplined, who managed their time efficiently, and who paced themselves well, were also the ones who were most effective at managing change over an extended period. The lesson is clear, and it is an aspect that should attract more importance at selection boards in future, since a leader who does not posses this level of self-discipline and maturity will only put more pressure on the rest of the team. In the past it was possible for the team to have the time to 'manage' this – but those days are gone.

■ The skills to win hearts and minds

The five behaviours of our sample CEOs above have also revealed certain skills required of 'change leaders'. These have embraced: setting clear direction; effectiveness as a communicator; releasing potential and creativity; delegation; and flexibility. In order to win the hearts and minds of followers, leaders need also to develop other skills.

The first is related to releasing potential and delegation – it is empowerment. Taken literally, this involves leaders totally trusting their people to take responsibility for their own actions. However, although many leaders understand the importance of empowerment, only a few appreciate how to achieve it. The key to this is good teamwork. The building of an effective team is a fundamental requirement of leadership, and it cannot be achieved overnight. It requires hard work, planning, energy, flexibility and resilience. Empowerment stems from the trust built over time through a team learning to work together. It needs to be nurtured and developed, and that requires patience and coaching. The latter is another fundamental skill of leadership and it has assumed more importance as organisations have downsized, developed flatter structures and 'inverted the triangle'. Indeed, it has become so important that the 'leader as coach' phrase has taken on greater significance. In order to achieve full empowerment, it is necessary for the leader to create the right environment, and then to coach people for their roles. Once again, this cannot be done quickly and, in most cases, it necessitates leaders learning how to become coaches themselves.

Coaching is also linked to the next skill, which is succession planning. The need to groom successors is an area with a mixed track record. The public sector, in general, is quite good at this and, for instance, the Civil Service and the military have an impressive record of selecting effective senior executives. The same cannot be said for the private sector, and even large companies have found this difficult (e.g., GEC and Marks & Spencer at the end of the 1990s). Identification and development of the next generation of leaders, at all levels, is a necessary skill for senior management in order to guarantee the continuation of the relevant organisation. However, there is more to it than this in today's environment because, in order to succeed, it is the continuation of ideas that is really important. This is only achieved through the development of a group of like-minded people who are encouraged to grow together, with the more experienced members bringing on the others. In such an environment, however, there can be a danger of 'cloning', which should be avoided.

It is important that there is an atmosphere of challenge and risk, so that the various contenders can be evaluated and tested. This is particularly apt when there is a group of good candidates all vying for selection (one of the reasons for the good record of the Civil Service and the military). A failure to have an effective succession plan can lead to loss of direction and a slowing-down of momentum, which could be disastrous in today's fast-moving world. On the other hand, the rewards can be great, as Ken Keir pointed out when he remarked on the satisfaction of seeing a young team, which he had selected and developed, who were really succeeding at senior management level.

Another skill which is particularly pertinent at senior level is that of boundary management. This involves both the time a leader spends on the external *versus* the internal; and also managing the 'boundaries' inside an organisation. Taking the internal/external aspect first, perhaps the first surprise for an individual appointed to chief executive level is the amount of time required to deal with external issues. Naturally, this depends on the nature of the job, however, it is not unusual to be required to attend two or three engagements a week, often in the evening, and frequently as the 'guest speaker'. These commitments are in addition to the normal requirements to deal with the external aspects of the job, which will include a good deal of networking. The latter is an essential part of communication at this level because it enables people to glean information, promote their own ideas, and also to cultivate allies. In effect, this represents team building at senior executive level.

With regard to managing boundaries inside an organisation, this requires a leader's antennae to be carefully tuned. In most companies, office politics are endemic and part of the background to the normal relationships which exist in any organisation. Even those which claim to be free of such a curse will find this rising to the surface as soon as there is a problem. Leaders need to be aware of the 'background noise' of the organisation, and move quickly to counter politically motivated activities and rumours which can, so easily, promote mischief. Quite often, this will not be malevolent but more likely will be caused by a feeling of uncertainty. Once again, the leader's role is to counter this through clear communication. It is a skill which is acquired through experience; it is time-consuming, tiring and requires patience. It is also essential.

The reader will have noticed that the subject of communication has reappeared. This is hardly surprising, since it is probably the most fundamental skill of all – and it covers such a large spectrum. There are two further aspects associated with communication to mention here. The first is for the leader to act as a 'communication agent'. This is especially important in continuous change because, in effective companies, there will be a number of ideas bubbling around the various divisions which can remain unconnected unless an attempt is made to co-ordinate them. This is the role of the leader. In particular, it requires an ability to be aware of what is happening in the divisions, followed by an analysis of the various ideas, and subsequently, co-ordination and alignment. The second aspect, which has been mentioned already, is that of listening. It is an essential skill of communication, and one that becomes more important, the higher one gets.

The last part of this section is about self. This is not about a skill: however, without this, the skills mentioned above would be meaningless. It embraces Daniel Goleman's key aspects of Emotional Intelligence[18] (self-confidence, maturity, self-awareness – and values). It is about all the ingredients that, together, make up the individual who is the leader. It is promoted by personal example, it is matured by experience, and it can be developed through learning. Above all, it is about beliefs and values. One can develop the necessary skills of leadership but without a strong sense of values it will not be possible to win the hearts and minds of people. Furthermore, these need to be transparent because they will be called into question frequently, and often without warning. This Values-Based Leadership is the foundation stone on which the skills are based.

So, there we have it – the skills required to win hearts and minds. To re-cap, they are:

- providing clear direction
- effectiveness as a communicator (including being a communication agent and a good listener)
- releasing potential and creativity
- delegation
- flexibility
- empowerment (including coaching and developing teamwork)
- succession planning
- boundary management (including the external/internal balance and the management of internal politics)
- and, of course – self.

■ Putting it all together

So far we have considered the necessary behaviours and skills which combine to enable leaders to win the hearts and minds of the people. In this final section we look at how this is all put together to achieve a critical mass in support of the change process.

The first point to emphasise is that leaders have to be Champions of Change. This can best be achieved by emphasising the positive aspects of change. It requires a constant optimistic approach and will necessitate endless discussions to counter the negative. It is exhausting and, at times, the leader will wonder whether it is worth continuing. When this depression is experienced, remember that all change leaders experience The Dark Night of the Innovator – when you think that it cannot possibly get worse, it will! As we saw in Chapter Four (Figure 4.3) this occurs at the bottom of the 'change curve', and it is a necessary part of the process. Indeed, until a leader has experienced this, they cannot be sure that the organisation has really started on the upward curve. The other point about concentrating on the positive is that it is an essential means of encouragement for those people who are supporters of the change process. They will need constant encouragement if they are to remain allies.

A clear strategy is an obvious requirement; however, achieving this in an environment of constant change is not easy. The problem is that the speed of change, often involving rapid technology developments, means that a particular strategy can become outdated quickly (for instance, the processing power of computers is doubling every eighteen months). It is therefore important to adopt a flexible attitude to strategy, and to be prepared to alter original thinking and adapt to changing circumstances. It is also important to include the contributions of all the relevant people within the organisation towards the development of strategy, as this will encourage a feeling of ownership.

This is a key aspect of the process and is therefore something which change leaders need to encourage and develop. One of the best ways to achieve this is to link the benefits of change with the strengths of the organisation in terms of where it will be in the 'new' position. This can be a most effective way of combating the fear of change which, inevitably, will be experienced by a number of people. To many of them, it will be the fear of uncertainty which will be the problem. The counter to this is to remove 'the uncertainty' early. In many circumstances, senior management will delay announcing a decision because of the implications for their employees when, in fact, the latter are well aware of the options, and would far rather be told the worst. Much better to know early that you have been made redundant than to wait for months in limbo – at least you can start making alternative plans.

We have already mentioned self-pacing, and this is equally important during the process. It is important to constantly review the procedures in order to assess the implications for people, and to ensure that everyone is able to cope with the pace of change. It will often be necessary to slow down the process to ensure that it is managed properly. Nobody should be under any illusion about the wearing aspect of constant change which can exhaust the most willing advocates. It is therefore clearly a leadership responsibility to ensure that people cope with this relentless pressure, and managers need to be prepared to relax the programme where appropriate and, above all, to adopt a flexible approach. The use of frequent reviews is an important part of this process.

The other crucial aspect of self-pacing is to achieve change by means of small steps. This is best done by chosing the easiest part first, by getting agreement from all those involved as to the best way to proceed – and then, when this part has been completed, to celebrate success. This is a well-proven approach but is so often forgotten in senior management's haste to achieve the required changes too quickly.

All of this involves sensitivity. Leaders need to be sensitive to both the pace of change and also the impact on their teams. Once again, it depends upon expertise in communication (particularly in listening) – but it also involves the ability to observe behaviour, and to take action or make decisions when necessary. This is all part of the caring aspect of leadership which all the best managers possess.

So, in summary, the key ingredients are:

■ championing change
■ a clear, but flexible, strategy
■ enthusiastic optimism
■ encouraging ownership
■ removing 'fear'
■ flexibility
■ emphasising the positive
■ effective communications
■ removing 'uncertainty' early

- holding frequent reviews
- aiming for small successes, step by step – and remembering to celebrate
- resilience
- sensitivity.

■ Summary

In this chapter we have considered the behaviours and skills required for the 'hearts and minds' of leadership. We have done this by drawing both on the experience of effective change leaders, and also on our own work in helping organisations to get the best from their people.

Winning hearts and minds of people is not easy. It requires energy and persistence, especially when the organisation is at the bottom of the 'change curve.' Being a change leader can also be a lonely position, which is one of the reasons for developing good teamwork, sharing the load and making the most of the available talent. The purpose is to release the potential of all the people in the organisation and to do it in such a way that the best of the old methods are balanced with the best of the new.

Finally, it is important to have fun. All of those to whom we talked were obviously enjoying what they were doing, and were also keen to see that their people enjoyed their work as well. This was best encapsulated by Sir Stuart Hampson in his observation that 'happiness is a fundamental objective of management'.[19] If people are happy in their work then they will perform consistently well. The key to winning hearts and minds is for the leader to create the right atmosphere for happiness to thrive.

Endnotes

1   IOD Survey (1998) *Sign of the Times*
2   Interview with John Roberts, 7 October 1998
3   Interview with Sir Paul Condon, 11 November 1998
4   Ken Keir, op.cit.
5   *People Management*, 4 December 1998
6   John Roberts, op.cit.
7   Interview with Gail Rebuck, 22 September 1998
8   Interview with Tim Melville-Ross, 12 August 1998
9   Interview with Jim Mowatt, 17 December 1998
10 Interview with Mair Barnes, 18 January 1999
11 Ken Keir, op.cit.

12   Sir Stuart Hampson, op.cit.

13   Interview with Leo McKee, 4 February 1999

14   Gail Rebuck, op.cit.

15   *The Times Magazine*, 1 October 1994

16   Mair Barnes, op.cit.

17   Sir Peter Davis, op.cit.

18   Daniel Goleman (1996), *Emotional Intelligence*, Bloomsbury

19   Sir Stuart Hampson, op.cit.

Appetiser

CHAPTER SEVEN

In this chapter, you will:

■ EXAMINE THE IDEA THAT 'STRATEGY' HAS, APPARENTLY, FALLEN OUT OF FAVOUR

■ FIND OUT ABOUT A RANGE OF STRATEGIC OPTIONS

■ REVISIT THE LEVELS OF LEADERSHIP AND THE ORGANISATIONAL CULTURE AS A BASIS FOR DEVELOPING STRATEGY

■ REALISE THAT LEADERS AT THE TOP OF ORGANISATIONS NEED TO BE REMINDED ABOUT THE REAL FRONT-LINE ISSUES

■ EXAMINE THE CASE FOR CREATING A STRATEGIC APPROACH IN UNCERTAIN TIMES

■ SEE THAT CREATING THE CONDITIONS FOR STRATEGY TO DEVELOP IS AS IMPORTANT AS THE STRATEGY ITSELF

■ BE INTRODUCED TO SOME SIMPLE TOOLS FOR DEVELOPING STRATEGIC CREATIVITY, INCLUDING EFFECTIVE GOAL-SETTING.

Crafting Effective Change Strategy

■ Strategy – why bother?

If there is one word that seems to be at the heart of both leadership and organisational life it is 'strategy'. The idea of having a grand plan to bring a vision into reality is fundamentally important to all organisations if they are to survive and develop. In the past three decades, we have seen a tremendous growth in 'the business of strategy'. High priced consultancy organisations offer tailormade solutions to businesses wanting to develop and grow, and there is a wealth of literature on the subject of business strategy in general. There is no doubt that this thinking has benefited many organisations worldwide, improving their ability not only to survive but to gain market share, to develop their portfolios of operations and to achieve high levels of success in a variety of ways.

Yet in some ways, the issue of strategy is now causing concern. To have a clear, well-formed strategy is to imply that you have concrete plans for the way ahead and that in some way you can both predict and control the future. We now live in such uncertain times that it could be argued that it is no longer viable to think in terms of creating a long-term plan. In fact, many business thinkers, including ourselves, would argue that even three years is a long time in the current world in which we live!

This idea of strategy being less useful than in the past is at odds with our ideas on leadership. Right at the top of our list of Leadership Competencies is the idea of setting direction, of creating the grand plan and bringing the vision into reality. We thus have a paradox. There is an obvious need to create direction. However, it is difficult to be firm about that direction because the situation is constantly changing. Many organisations seem to respond to this paradox by focusing on short-term operational effectiveness rather than trying to create a longer-term, more strategic approach to their operations. And there are sound reasons for taking this course of action. The financial world constantly seeks good returns on investment in the short term and share prices are often closely linked to operational performance and short-term results.

Secondly, it is much easier to justify time and resources invested in optimising processes in a business through continuous improvement initiatives and maximising operating efficiencies than it is to rationalise taking time out for some 'blue sky' strategic thinking. Yet it is that 'blue sky' thinking approach that leads to results in the future direction of the organisation and its ultimate success or failure.

Thirdly, many would argue that in an uncertain world, what is the point of planning anyway? Surely it is better to respond to demands as they arise rather than to invest resources into creating a strategy which may become redundant overnight as a result of some changing external factor, such as a new competitor or a technological breakthrough.

It is this sort of thinking that has led to a lessening in popularity of taking a strategic approach, particularly in the business world. In our view it is a dangerous approach.

In this chapter, we are going to look at strategy from the leadership viewpoint and outline a number of practical approaches to enable effective change to take place. We believe that a balanced approach to strategy is needed. We are living in times of accelerating change and only the naïve beginner would attempt to create a rigid five-year or ten-year plan which would be adhered to in every detail. Vision needs to take into account that the situation will alter in today's environment of constant change. This will almost certainly result in strategies becoming redundant or inappropriate. This means that we have to take a more comprehensive look at strategy to provide ourselves with more options at key decision points. So, an important feature of this chapter is that it is the range of strategic approaches which is the most significant factor, rather than a specific strategy in its own right which is important.

So if strategy is such a contentious issue, why should we bother with trying to create plans for the future? Perhaps this question is best answered by Arie de Geus in his book *The Living Company*.[1]

Arie de Geus was the Head of Scenario Planning for the Shell Oil Company for many years. This role involved running a team of researchers whose prime job was to create stories of possible future directions in which the world may change so that the company could predict its future, and so make wiser business decisions. One of the most powerful points made by de Geus is that the lifespan of the average corporation is relatively short. He quotes the fact that if you check the names of the companies featured in the Fortune 500 list in 1970, one-third had vanished by 1983 due to takeovers, mergers and liquidations. So de Geus asked himself what characteristics were featured in organisations that did survive for many years, sometimes centuries, as in the case of the Stora company or Sumitomo.

He found that long-lasting companies who had identified that their main objective was to survive and reach their potential had four main features: they were sensitive to the changes taking place around them, they had a cohesive sense of corporate identity, they tolerated experiments at the margin of the enterprise and they were financially conservative. As a starting point for creating both the conditions for the development of strategy and the strategy itself, these four areas seem to be useful.

Strategy has to take into account a viewpoint of the future and we can identify basic scenarios for any organisation. Firstly, the future may be clearly identified. For example, a new technological development in electronics may mean that a manufacturing company might have to reassess its market position, how it organises production and how it supports its products post sale. For this type of predictable future situation, creating a strategy is a matter of applying well-tried tools such as SWOT analysis (strengths, weaknesses, opportunities and threats) and process mapping to create an integrated response to the new.

The second type of future scenario is when two or more clearly identifiable options exist. For example, a business organisation might want to expand its operations and enter new markets. Should it focus on these markets on a national basis, on a specific area of the world (say Asia or South America) or should it attempt to develop in several areas at once? Each possible future has pros and cons, and the strategic process tends to be one of decision-making between the alternatives, taking into account external factors which might alter the relative attractiveness of each possible scenario.

A third type of future scenario involves a complete range of options rather than one or two specific alternatives. This could mean up to nine or ten possible directions, many of which overlap to create a great deal of uncertainty. An example might be a company currently operating on a national basis wanting to develop an international business. Which countries do they target? Do they target one country per continent or every country in just one continent? The range of possibilities is enormous.

The fourth and final scenario we have identified is where there is total ambiguity. The organisation can go in any direction. An example of this might be a venture capital company which has a significant amount of money to invest. Does it target the financial sector, communications, the computer industry, manufacturing or space exploration? The range of possibilities is infinite and represents a truly ambiguous situation. It is important to identify the nature of the future facing the organisation because this influences directly the approach required to create both the conditions for strategy to emerge and the strategy itself.

However, before looking at both of these issues, we need to revisit our basic idea in Chapter One that we see three distinct levels of leadership process taking place in the organisation.

■ The three levels of leadership process revisited

We have already identified in Chapter One the three levels of leadership: the strategic, operational and front-line levels. However, before looking at the nature of the strategic process of leadership, it is useful at this stage to remind ourselves of the three levels of leadership activity and a convenient way to do this is to consider the diagram in Figure 7.1. We can see that the strategic level is about vision, purpose or mission, values and communication of those aspects of the organisation. The operational level is more concerned with implementing the strategy by the effective use of human energy on a day-to-day basis. Such issues as management style, the amount of coaching that takes place and the general atmosphere and climate of the organisation are significant at this operational level.

Robert Simons and Antonio Davila have addressed the issue of management energy in a very useful article in the *Harvard Business Review*.[2] They argue that whilst the classic performance measuring ratios for businesses usually involve such measurements as return on equity, return on assets and return on sales, perhaps the most useful may be to reflect how well the organisation implements its strategy. Their suggestion is that return on management time and energy is a key determinant of whether or not the organisation is effective in turning strategy into action, and they have

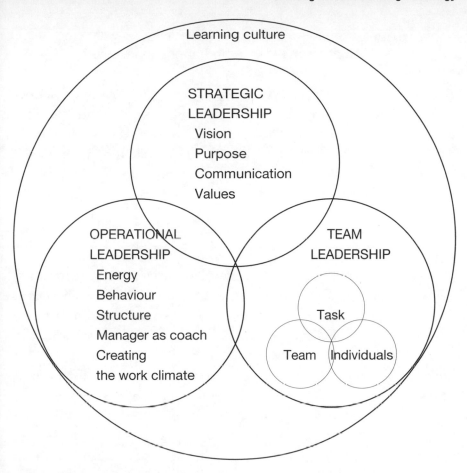

LEADERSHIP AT ALL LEVELS

Creating direction

Acting as an example

Communicating effectively

Getting the best out of people

Creating emotional alignment

Acting as a change agent

Handling the crisis

Figure 7.1 A model of the organisation

suggested that there is a ratio which measures this called ROM (return on management):

$$\text{ROM} = \frac{\text{Productive organisational energy released}}{\text{Management time and attention invested}}$$

This idea of management energy corresponds very closely with our idea of emotional alignment, because it reinforces the idea that the prime role of the manager is to achieve results through both their own efforts and those of their colleagues. The extent to which this happens is dictated by the amount of directed energy which people put into their work. It is not just a case of working harder but of identifying the key issues that warrant energy and effort being put into them. This idea will be considered again later in this chapter when we explore the idea of the Balanced Scorecard.

The third level of leadership process we have identified is the front-line or team leadership level. This is where groups of individuals are organised as teams either in a production or a service context. Usually the boundaries of the task are clearly defined. It may be a production cell in a manufacturing plant where the cell leader is responsible for, say, ten individuals who have to produce a specific quota of work output to a defined quality standard. Or it may be a customer helpdesk type situation where a team of individuals represent the organisation to the customer in terms of after-sales service.

The context of the front-line situation does not matter. It is the attitude of mind of the individuals operating within this team situation which is the important factor, and this is defined more by the impact of their leader than almost anything else. We only have to travel on several flights with the same airline to realise that it is rare to receive exactly the same quality of service from different workteams. The key factor in determining the quality of service is usually the leadership ability of the purser, chief flight attendant or in some cases the captain of the aircraft, depending on the airline.

At this front-line level, it is possible to achieve dramatic performance improvement by simply developing the action-centred approach of Professor John Adair.[3] In this very practical approach to understanding how leaders should operate, attention is placed on the needs of the task, the needs of the team undertaking the task as a team and the specific needs of individuals within the team.

In fact it is really the impact of the strategic leadership at the front-line level which is, perhaps, the ultimate test of effective leadership at the top. If you ask the average person in the street the name of the Postmaster-General in their country, or the name of the regional head of the postal service, they

almost certainly will not be able to answer you. And probably they do not care who those individuals are. What they do care about, however, is the attitude of the person behind the counter in their local post office and the person who delivers the mail. This is true for almost every business organisation. The ultimate judgement is made during what Jan Carlzon of SAS called the 'Moments of Truth'.[4]

When Carlzon inherited SAS, it was making a substantial loss. In just a year he turned the business around so that it was well into profit. He did this through the idea of looking at the interactions between staff and customers as the prime shaper of the corporate image rather than the more conventional approach of logos, corporate identity and developing physical assets. His argument was that as SAS carried around 10 million passengers each year and on average each passenger came into contact with five members of the airline staff, the key to success was the effective management of these 50 million 'Moments of Truth'. In many respects, Carlzon was the forerunner of the present interest in the concept of intellectual capital as different from physical capital in a business.

■ How do we assess the impact of effective leadership on the front line?

We have noticed a fascinating trend in relation to these three levels of leadership process and how they may be integrated in the real world. In many organisations there has been a feeling in the past that the management at the top is divorced from the front-line issues. Many organisational leaders have worked hard at addressing this issue. Several years ago, Tom Peters cited the example of the President of the Sony Corporation spending several months of each year touring retail outlets for the Sony product range and actually working on the counter in stores selling the products to real customers. This is a trend that has reasserted itself in recent years as business leaders struggle hard to identify how they can improve the effectiveness of their organisations.

We encountered two very interesting examples of this interest by business leaders in returning to the basic delivery function of the organisation. Firstly, Terry Brown, a millionaire running the holiday company Unijet, recently spent a week working as a holiday tour representative at one of the locations where his company organises holidays. Brown, the Managing Director of Unijet, was featured in a BBC documentary programme 'Back to the Floor' where managing directors and chief executives voluntarily work for a period of time on the front line of their organisations, whether they be service or manufacturing. Brown experienced many of the trials and tribulations of his front-line workers first hand, including dealing with hostile passengers who were subject to airport delays. As a result of his experience on the front line, Brown has been able to implement a number of minor changes in the way Unijet operates. Individually, none of the changes were earth-shattering, but taken together they have enabled Unijet and its employees to perform more effectively and gain more enjoyment from their work.

Another example of the 'Back to the Floor' principle featured a utility company in the West of England. South-West Water, a subsidiary of Pennon Group Plc, had a troubled history in the 1990s including pollution incidents, poor public perception (partly as a result of having the country's highest water and sewerage charges) and a number of other issues. The result was a company which was not only moving from the public sector to the private sector, but doing so in an increasingly restricted and regulated environment with a poor public image and a de-motivated workforce.

The Chief Executive, Bob Baty, with many years' experience in the water industry, chose to spend a week working on the front line with his inspectors and their teams. This involved responding to a variety of incidents and dealing with irate customers who could not see why they should pay high charges for water and sewerage services in a geographical area known for its significantly high annual rainfall.

Baty had two objectives in mind when he undertook his 'Back to the Floor' exercise. Firstly there was the education issue of why the company had to charge relatively high amounts of money for its services. Issues such cleaning up many old crude sewage discharge pipes along a large area of coastline, a huge programme to replace old water supply pipes and poor facilities and the sheer geographical size of South-West Water's operating area all needed to be spelled out to the customers.

Secondly, there was a perceived gap between the senior management of the company and the front-line staff and workers. By spending time with a range of his front-line operators, Baty was able to do much to close the perceived gap. Whilst the organisation is not perfect yet, it has moved dramatically towards a more positive public profile and a healthier climate within, particularly in the middle-management levels. Talking about his experience on the front line, Bob Baty clearly felt it was very worthwhile and that it taught him more than any management course could have ever achieved.

The lesson from these examples is that it is not what happens at the top that matters but the way the organisation operates to develop excellence in terms of front-line delivery of its products and services.

A fascinating approach to the challenge of motivating the front line is given by Jon Katzenbach and Jason Santamaria in their article 'Firing up the front-line' in a recent issue of the *Harvard Business Review*.[5] Both authors argue that, for many organisations, achieving competitive advantage means that the front line delivery process of the product or service is the ultimate discriminator between the successful and the mediocre. They cite as a powerful example the impact on the front line of effective leadership processes with a research project carried out by a team of McKinsey researchers. These researchers decided to explore the 'mission, values and pride' approach of the US Marine Corps to assess its relevance to the business world. The authors discovered that although there are critical differences between the Marines and the business world, there were five factors that were transferable.

Firstly, the Marines over-invest in cultivating core values. Secondly, they prepare every person to lead, whatever their predicted rank. Thirdly, every individual learns the importance of the correct timing of either creating a team approach or as single-leader workgroups, depending on which is most appropriate in the situation. This is important as it further points to the suggestion that the consensus team approach is not always the answer to every problem encountered in the workplace. Fourthly, all employees attract attention, not just the high performers. Finally, self-discipline is encouraged as a way of building pride. Although self-discipline seems to be somewhat out of favour in modern society, it is interesting to reflect that individuals, both in effective leadership positions and as effective followers, tend to achieve better results in what they undertake when they adhere to their values and follow a disciplined approach to behaviour. This was also a factor identified in the last chapter under 'Self-pacing'.

■ The importance of a constructive organisational culture

Returning to our three levels of leadership, it is important to realise that these take place within the cultural setting of the organisation. It is the culture of the organisation which determines the extent to which leadership is enabled or inhibited on a day-to-day basis. In 'flat' organisations where empower-ment is part of the ethos, a significant amount of leadership tends to be found at all levels, including the front line. In contrast, in hierarchical and bureaucratic settings, leadership tends to be stifled with few individuals taking personal ownership of problem situations.

■ The three levels and enabling effective change to take place

If we now relate this to strategy, successful change strategy should involve all three of the leadership levels plus an assessment and (usually) development of the culture towards a more enabling environment for leadership to emerge at the three levels. Culture does not just affect the front line and the middle management but also the directors, vice-presidents and the senior management team as a whole. In fact the way that the individuals in senior leadership positions within the organisation behave towards each other and to the workforce are the key determinants of culture, particularly with regard to the extent to which communications are open, and also the amount of energy which is wasted on internal politics. In creating a strategy, therefore, we need to ensure that all four areas are taken into account: the three levels of leadership and the cultural backdrop.

Not only does there need to be a clear vision and sense of purpose, but the strategy must be capable of being turned into action in a way that harnesses management energy, and then inspires the front line to want to deliver high quality results in a positive, creative and innovative way. At the same time the culture needs to enable creativity, growth, innovation and leadership to develop.

We will now start to address the nature of strategy, bearing in mind this four-part framework.

In recent years there seems to have been a marked reduction in the effort which organisations have been investing into the creation of effective strategy. Perhaps this is one of the reasons why there seems to be such a need for leadership in all our organisations. Thinking has simply become reactive, short-term and expedient, rather than strategic and far-seeing. Michael de Kare-Silver makes this point in his book *Strategy in Crisis*.[6] He points to the enormous increase in competition which all business organisations are experiencing, and the quality of strategic thinking that is needed to cope with this trend is making some harsh distinctions between the winners and the losers. On one hand we have observed the difficulties that established giants such as IBM and GM have experienced during the past decade, whilst at the same time there are some real winners such as Procter & Gamble, WalMart and British Airways. De Kare-Silver makes the statement that 'occasionally leaders emerge with the guts and determination to drive through change, who have become committed to a strategy and the way forward and who are prepared to break down walls to get there'. There is a strong link between leadership and strategy; and any book on effective change leadership needs to explore and develop this link.

For many organisations, strategy and planning are seen as the same thing and revolve around setting budgets. This is akin to saying that business success can only be measured in financial terms. As recent examples in the business world have shown, this is far from the truth, and devices such as the Balanced Scorecard are an attempt to break away from the limited, purely financial viewpoint.

Strategies for the future need to be different from the past and leaders must take this into account, whatever their area of operation.

Firstly, there has been a definite shift in power from the producer to the customer. Organisations that ignore this fact do so at their own peril. Secondly, as Tom Peters has said on many occasions, 'Big is not necessarily beautiful.' In particular, niche markets are often best supplied by small, extremely responsive business units who are totally focused on their needs and who avoid bureaucratic operation like the plague. The global spread of operations and the dissolution of all sorts of boundaries place a tremendous need to adapt on all organisations. Multicultural working and diversity issues now assume a greater level of importance than ever before.

Technology, in particular information technology, is opening doors to markets that have never before been a serious target. Eastern Europe, South Africa, Asia all have become more significant than we would have ever anticipated. At the same time, new, low-cost competition is increasing daily, meaning that all organisations are having to take their competitive position very seriously.

That is the stuff of strategy and the problem is that many of the tools that business leaders have used in the past are simply not as appropriate today as when they were conceived in the more stable world of the 1960s and 1970s. Such tools as the Boston Matrix, Product Impact of Market Strategy (PIMS), Porter's Five Forces and Three Generic Strategies of lowest cost, differenti- **159** ation and niche focus, and Hamel and Prahalad's Core Competencies[7] have all been useful in their time and can still play a part in the formulation of strategy. However, each approach has both strengths and weaknesses and the interested reader is referred to de Kare-Silver's excellent summary of these and other approaches.

■ Does strategy need to be simple or complex?

The subject of strategy can be made as simple or as complex as required. Henry Mintzberg and Joseph Lampel[8] have suggested that there are ten schools of strategy. Three of these schools are prescriptive and are based on the ideas of designing, of planning and of positioning. The authors consider each of these three approaches in terms of the source of each approach to strategy, the base discipline, its champions, its intended and realised messages, and associated homilies such as 'Look before you leap', 'Nothin' but the facts' and so on. The other approaches are what the authors call 'descriptive', describing things as they are rather than as what they ought to be. These include entrepreneurial vision, cognitively based approaches, experimentation and learning, gaining power, cultural fit, environmental fit and configuration.

Whilst it could be argued that some of these divisions overlap and are somewhat artificial, they do point to the fact that strategy can be made into a very complex science! The danger is, of course, that the design process becomes so complex that little in the way of implementation occurs. Indeed the final point made by the authors is that what we really need is the ability to ask better questions and generate fewer hypotheses to create better practice, not more elegant theory.

■ Strategy and the future

What now seems to be emerging is that strategy formulation in the future will have to take into account the changing environment in which the organisation is operating more comprehensively than ever before. In particular, the importance of a strategic approach to developing intellectual capital is likely to become increasingly important in the next few decades. As we are moving from the age of the importance of financial capital to the age of the importance of intellectual capital and knowledge, how does this fundamental shift impact on the need and process for developing strategy?

One approach to crafting effective strategy for the future is outlined by de Kare-Silver. His 'Market Commitment' model identifies, for example, four prime axes of competitive advantage surrounding a core of commitment. The four prime competencies are 'service hustle', 'price', 'performance' and 'emotion'. Once again we see the emergence of the 'E' word, as it is known. At last we are acknowledging that human beings are emotional animals and that once again is a pointer to the importance of effective leadership, which is so strongly linked to the harnessing of emotional energy.

It has often been said that strategy is the first step we take in order to turn a policy into actual operations. For many years the business literature has published a tremendous amount of material on strategy, particularly in the financial and the marketing areas. However, in the latter part of the twentieth century there seems almost to have been an abandonment of strategy on the basis that there is no point trying to predict the future with five-year or ten-year strategic plans, because in a few months the world can change dramatically, rendering such plans useless.

■ Do we really want to create strategy or the conditions for it to emerge?

Gary Hamel has addressed this issue in an article for the *Sloan Management Review*.[9] He argues that rather than try to create strategy, we should focus on creating the prerequisites for strategy to emerge as the scenario changes. His point is really summed up in the following quote: '. . . in a discontinuous world, strategy innovation is the key to wealth creation . . .' So rather than talk in terms of creating strategy, the focus is on creating an environment in which strategy can emerge and grow as the organisation continually re-invents itself to deal with its changing environment.

Hamel suggests firstly that strategy should not just be the province of top management but that other people, including front-line individuals and the more youthful element of the organisation, should be allowed to voice their opinions. This reflects the idea of Rosabeth Kanter's 'Council of Youth' in the organisation.[10] Many organisations have their 'Council of Elders' which, Kanter suggests, should work with the younger element rather than ignore them. Perhaps strategy should take into account both the energy of youth and the wisdom of age![11]

Hamel's second point is that new communication processes need to be created which are cross-departmental and even cross-industry in order to avoid falling into the trap of the same people talking about the same issues in the same meetings. It is very easy for patterns to emerge which gradually dissolve any possibility of creative thinking and these patterns need to be broken if true strategic creativity is to be achieved.

Creating a sense of passion for change is Hamel's third point. He argues that individuals are only against change when it doesn't offer any new opportunity or benefit to them individually. Once again we can see the importance of the emotion aspect arising, this time in terms of the idea of a return on emotional investment. People will invest emotional energy in the change when there's a chance to create a unique and exciting future in which they can share.

New perspectives are vital if an organisation is to create the conditions for creative strategy to emerge and this is Hamel's fourth point. It is important to reassess areas such as customer issues, employee issues and the organisation's capabilities on a regular basis to enable the organisation to re-invent itself.

Finally we have the notion of new experiments. This involves launching a series of small risk-avoiding experiments in the market to see which strategies will work and which will not.

Table 7.1 Creating the conditions for effective strategy to emerge

1. Involve everybody at all levels within the organisation. This is particularly true for individuals at the front line who may have to implement the strategy in terms of changing the way they work.

2. Promote effective communication, both inside the organisation in cross-functional terms and in terms of outside networking. Becoming sensitive to the outside world and its changes is key to creating effective strategy.

3. Create a passion for change. Sell people on the benefits of doing things differently to produce better results. Remove as much as possible of the fear of the uncertainty about the way ahead.

4. Gain new perspectives on your capabilities and market needs. View your products, services and operations from as many viewpoints as possible: customers, suppliers, employees, local community, trade associations and the other stakeholders who have an interest in the survival of your organisation.

5. Carry out small minimal risk experiments at the margins of your operation to try out new things to see what will work in the future.

Strategy is therefore about creating the conditions for its emergence as much as it is about creating rigid strategic plans. However, we do need to have some idea of our intended direction or else we will simply dissipate our energy and our resources, and eventually cease to exist. We also do need to have some idea of where we are going, whilst at the same time being aware of the results we are creating, and then adjust both our strategy and our performance accordingly.

We have combined Hamel's ideas with our own experience on how to create the optimal conditions for strategy to emerge, and the result is shown in Table 7.1.

■ Creating strategy – a basic approach

The starting point for creating change is straightforward. It is about deciding where you are at present, then creating a vision for the future, and thirdly, designing a process to get you there. We will start with the present position.

There are a number of useful and simple to use tools to help us create a strategy for change. First we will consider ways of evaluating our current position. Perhaps the most widely know of these tools is the SWOT analysis – strengths, weaknesses, opportunities and threats. The first two factors relate to the internal characteristics of the organisation and the second to external factors which will be likely to impact on the organisation. A straightforward brainstorming process is used to identify all the strengths that the organisation is seen to possess and these are noted on a flipchart. From this list (which will probably be substantial), the most significant ones are chosen as key areas to build on in terms of the organisation's position in the marketplace.

The second exercise is to plot the weaknesses of the organisation. This list is not usually so substantial but is important in that it can identify internal factors which are potentially likely to limit progress. There is an argument that we should actually ignore weaknesses on the basis that the more you think about something the more likely you are to bring that issue into reality! However, we believe it is important that potential weaknesses are identified, even if the linguistics are changed and they are referred to as 'areas for development' or 'what's not perfect yet'. Although this change in language may seen inconsequential, we should remind ourselves of Jay Conger's Persuasive Leadership which stresses the point that the style and type of words a leader uses are important in terms of creating the right impact on the followers and their subsequent behaviour. Using 'areas for development', for example, leads people forward into ways to improve things rather than wallowing in the 'mental mud' of despondency.

The external factors of opportunities and threats are self-explanatory and again these would be plotted on a flipchart. The most significant factors are then identified and these can lead to a strategy based on the idea of capitalising on strengths and taking advantage of opportunities, whilst at the same time being aware of the areas where things need to improve internally and the possible threats in the external environment and marketplace.

The idea of internal and external factors has been used most successfully by a number of strategic business advisers. Tony Everett is one such adviser (operating primarily in the South-West of England), who has a wealth of experience helping small and medium enterprises develop their levels of competitiveness. Everett first asks the management team to identify internal factors within the business which will impact on their ability to perform well in the future. Such factors may include quality of staff, motivation of the management team and sound positive cash flow. The same process is then used, this time to identify external factors which it is thought will impact on the operation. Such issues as competition, the Internet, customer expectations, changes in buying habits and changes in legislation usually arise here. Participants are then asked to identify the top five internal factors and the top five external factors and these are plotted on a grid as in Figure 7.2.

Each cell is then given a score based on the extent to which the relevant internal and external factors are related. A high relationship would attract a

EXTERNAL FACTORS

		Factor One	Factor Two	Factor Three	Factor Four	Factor Five
	Factor One					
INTERNAL	Factor Two					
FACTORS	Factor Three					
	Factor Four					
	Factor Five					

Figure 7.2 The internal-external factor matrix

score of 2, a medium to low relationship a score of 1 and little or no relationship would attract a zero. For example say internal factor 1 is ability to use information technology effectively and that external factor 1 was the increasing amount of business arising *via* the Internet, then these factors have a high impact on each other and would attract a 2. If however, internal factor 2 was quality of staff and external factor 4 was new legislation on waste disposal, then this would probably only attract a 1 or more likely a 0.

Once all the cells are filled, then the rows are totalled and the columns totalled.

The scores for each external factor and each internal factor are then ranked and the top six scores chosen to form the basis of the strategy. This is then represented on a fishbone diagram for clarity such as in Figure 7.3.

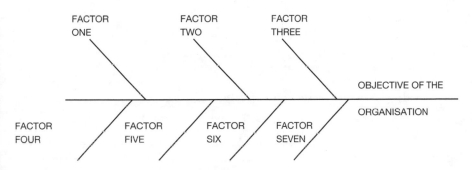

Figure 7.3 The strategic fishbone diagram

Simple graphical devices such as the fishbone diagram are useful in distilling thought and in ensuring that everyone is aware of both the strategic direction and the key areas where effort is needed to ensure that the organisation achieves its vision.

■ Strategic creativity

One of the major stumbling blocks for senior management teams in terms of their strategic ability is usually their lack of creativity. By lack of creativity we mean a lack of ability to create both the conditions for the emergence of strategy and also the creative quality of that strategy. It is our belief that it is the very route through which most senior executives have travelled in order to gain senior positions within the organisation that is their major obstacle.

In basic psychological terms it has been accepted for many years that human thought processes can conveniently be divided into two general types – left brain and right brain. In the business world, left brain or logical, analytical thinking is usually better rewarded, certainly in the short term. The irony is that it is right brain, creative, off-the-wall thinking that so frequently produces the best results in the long term. So, in understanding how to create both the conditions for the emergence of creative strategy and the quality of the strategy itself, what senior executives need to do is to let go and relax. This can be quite a challenging process for many, particularly for the so-called anal retentive personality who is locked into obeying the rules and not upsetting the corporate applecart! However, the future is not going to be like the past. It is the very process of challenging 'sacred cows' that so often brings about the outstanding ideas so craved by every corporation.

■ The power of a compelling vision

The starting point for creating effective strategy has to be the visioning process. Strategy really only works effectively when it is focused on bringing a vision or compelling picture of the future into reality. We now have a practical toolkit in terms of how we can develop our ability to create an effective vision. Neuro-Linguistic Programming (NLP) has given us an insight into the idea that human beings create internal representations of the world around them in three main ways: seeing, hearing and feeling. These three sensory modes can be divided into submodalities or specific details of an internal thought process. For example, the idea of the visual mode or internal picture we create of a situation is that it may be in colour or black and white, it may be still or moving, two-dimensional or panoramic.

Whatever our primary way of creating an internal representation of a situation, we have control over the specific details of that internal map. NLP is a powerful psychological technology which undoubtedly has much to offer in terms of understanding more about how to develop an effective visioning process. Joseph O'Connor and John Seymour explain this well in their excellent book Introducing NLP.[12]

■ The Balanced Scorecard

There is no doubt that the subject of strategy can be ill-defined with regard to the underpinning knowledge and process involved. It is not a science, nor is it exact in terms of there being a right or wrong way of how to create both the conditions for the emergence of effective strategy and the strategy itself. However, to conclude this chapter, it is useful to refer to the work of Robert Kaplan and David Norton with their idea of the Balanced Scorecard.[13]

These writers remind us of the adage 'what gets measured gets done' and that measuring success in a business is not just about short-term financial numbers. Kaplan and Norton suggest that the starting point for the Balanced Scorecard is the creation of a vision and then a strategy to bring that vision into reality. They suggest that the strategy should address four key issues:

■ financial issues (such as return on capital, cash flow, profitability and reliability)
■ customer issues (such as value for money, relationships and innovation)
■ internal issues (such as quality and project management)
■ growth issues (such as continuous improvement and developing the workforce)

Each of these areas is taken in turn and specific perspectives for each of the four areas are then examined. As a result of these perspectives, critical success factors are then identified which will show the extent to which the organisation is succeeding in each area. These critical success factors are then measured with key performance indicators which provide an easy, visual guide to performance. The exact style of the Balanced Scorecard produced for each organisation will obviously vary. However, it is the process chain of vision, strategy, strategic perspective areas, critical success factors and key performance indicators which provide the valuable contribution to our thought on strategy and its implementation.

Strategic goal-setting

Strategy on its own is worthless unless it can be turned into positive action. One of the key ways this may be accomplished is through the process of strategic goal-setting.

For many years, goal-setting has been recognised as a key skill for effective managers and leaders. It is vitally important in transforming strategy from esoteric ideas into practical action. This theme was recently reflected by Jim Collins in the *Harvard Business Review*.[14] Collins argues that although many leaders and senior executives have 'big, hairy, audacious goals (BHAGs)' many fail to turn them into tangible results because they lack a catalytic mechanism. Catalytic mechanisms are designed to ensure things happen rather than create bureaucracy. They tend to benefit the whole organisation rather than one element and often cause discomfort to those who traditionally hold power. They usually have what Collins calls 'teeth'. For example, there are often specific penalties such as bonuses linked to quality and punishments for lateness at meetings. To make a BHAG work, it is important to ensure that the organisation attracts the right people. It is not just that 'people are our most important asset' but that 'the right people are our most important asset'. Negative attitudes and people need to be weeded out. The final element of Collins' catalytic mechanisms is that an ongoing effect should be created, not just one or two events such as a speech or an off-site meeting. The important thing is to create momentum.

So if it is important to create 'big, hairy, audacious goals' and then ensure we have the catalytic mechanisms to ensure that they are translated into reality, how do we go about setting goals to ensure that they do work?

Tables 7.2 and 7.3 give some ideas on how we can approach the goal-setting process.

Table 7.2 Some ideas for strategic goal-setting

1. Decide what you want – be SMART (Specific, measurable, attainable, realistic/relevant and time-bounded).

2. Write down your goals in a matrix (areas/timescales).

3. Cycle your goals through the 'power questions'.

4. Decide the price you're prepared to pay to reach the goal.

5. Make a written project plan for each goal, working backwards to identify the tasks and stages.

6. Do something to start the ball rolling as soon as possible.

7. Anticipate potential barriers to achieving the goal and decide how you will deal with these barriers.

8. Visualise what achieving the goal would be like in terms of what you would see, hear and feel.

9. Check your progress and make appropriate adjustments. At each decision point, ask yourself if your proposed course of action will take you towards or away from your goal.

10. Review your goal matrix regularly.

11. Focus on the end point, not the process.

12. Remember the Laws of Belief, Expectations, Attraction and Correspondence. If we believe strongly enough in a goal we can achieve it, we produce what we expect to produce, we attract what we think about constantly and we need to be consistent in terms of what we say we are going to do and our actual behaviour.

Table 7.3 The differences between effective and ineffective goals

EFFECTIVE GOALS	INEFFECTIVE GOALS
Indicate how much is to be accomplished and how well it is to be accomplished	Do not specify any standards of performance
Are measurable in terms of quality and quantity	Are vague and unspecified
Indicate who is primarily responsible to ensure that it is achieved	Omit placing responsibility on anyone
Forecast an end result	Describe an activity without specifying an end result
Are clear and unambiguous	Are open to misinterpretation
Make it clear when the end result is to be achieved	Are open-ended and without any time limit
Are realistic, i.e., can be achieved 100%, taking all the circumstances of the situation into account, and the authority and ability of the person concerned	Are set unrealistically high, i.e., can't be achieved in the circumstances
Are challenging, likely to stretch people	Are likely to be achieved with minimum effort
Are of sufficient magnitude to cover several 'action steps' and extraneous influences	Are merely 'action steps'

Why should we set goals?

It does seem that people who set goals achieve more, yet it is probable that fewer than 5% of business executives set written goals and even then fewer than 1% achieve those goals. If we acknowledge that goal-setting is important in providing motivation and measurement, why is it that people seem to be so reluctant to set specific goals?

We have encountered a number of issues and they are frequently highlighted by statements such as:

'I've done OK without setting written goals'

'If I set a goal I may fail'

'Of course I have goals – in my head'

'If I achieve the goal I'll have to live up to it'

'I set goals when I need to'

'Goal-setting is OK for major tasks'

'Goals restrict freedom'

Whilst these are convenient excuses for not setting goals, they are an anathema to effective leadership. Goal-setting works and is a vital component of the strategy-setting process. We will look now at how we may develop a practical goal-setting process.

The principles of goal-setting

The first stage in effective goal-setting is to engage in some 'blue sky' thinking. Robert Schiller, the well-known evangelist, calls this 'possibility' thinking. It is about considering all the possibilities regardless of their practicality. A convenient way to approach blue sky thinking is to consider if anything were possible, what would you like to be, to do and to have, both in terms of resources and outcomes. The idea is to make three lists and then select from these three lists up to seven key goal issues.

Once this has been completed, it is then a question of creating a goal matrix, partly to build in timescales for the goals and partly to ensure that the goals do not conflict in any way with each other. (See Figure 7.4).

Once the goal matrix is created, then we cycle each of the goals through the power questions in Table 7.4 which build in both the ideas of SMART goals and of vision, that is, what we would see, hear and feel once the goal

is realised.

ACTIVITY AREA	1	2	3	4	5	6	7
TIMESCALE							
1 month							
3 months							
6 months							
1 year							
3 years							
5 years							
10 years							
Life							

Figure 7.4 The goal matrix

Table 7.4 The power questions for effective goal-setting

- What do I want to achieve?
- How can I create two ways of representing my goal visually (e.g., affirmation cards) to support my goal-related activity?
- Why do I want to achieve this goal?
- How can I give myself real leverage to achieve the goal?
- What benefits would I gain by achieving the goal?
- What pain would I avoid by achieving the goal?
- When do I want to achieve it?
- Is it realistic and relevant?
- Is it attainable?
- If I had achieved it what would I see?
- If I had achieved it what would I hear?
- If I had achieved it what sensations would I experience externally?
- How would I feel internally?
- How specifically will I go about the task? (Tip – work backwards)
- What first action step can I take right now?

- Why have I not achieved this goal yet?

- What roadblocks can I anticipate along the way and how will I deal with them?

- Which of my personal qualities do I need to strengthen in order to reach the goal?

- Do I really want to achieve this goal?

- Who else will it affect?

- What resources will I need?

Summary

In this chapter we have asked the question 'why bother about strategy?' The answer has to be that it is the key to both the survival and the growth of the organisation. In terms of longevity, it is vital for organisations to be aware of what is happening around them and how they can adapt to their changing environment, whilst at the same time retaining a cohesive identity. Furthermore, it is not simply a question of talking about or even creating strategy. Instead, it is about realising that there are three levels of process involved: creating the strategic direction, implementing the components of that strategic direction and impacting on the front line of the business in terms of attitudes, beliefs and quality of activity.

The importance of a constructive culture to enable these processes to develop has been discussed, together with a view that we are now moving from the 'Financial Capital' Age to the 'Intellectual and Knowledge Capital' Age. The strategic process is made up from two distinct aspects: creating the right conditions for strategy to emerge and be developed; and then the process of creating the strategy itself. We have presented some basic tools which will help develop both creativity and strategic vision, and also suggested how the various aspects of strategic thought may be fitted together in an integrated manner of which the Balanced Scorecard is one approach.

In the next chapter, we will explore the issue of evaluating success.

Endnotes

1 Arie de Geus, (1999), *The Living Company*, Nicholas Brealey
2 'How High is Your Return on Management?' *Harvard Business Review*, January–February 1998
3 John Adair (1983), *Effective Leadership*, Gower

4   Jan Carlzon (1987), Moments of Truth, HarperCollins

5   Jon. R. Katzenbach & Jason A. Santamaria 'Firing up the Front Line', Harvard Business Review, May–June 1999

6   Michael de Kare-Silver (1997), Strategy in Crisis, Macmillan

7   Gary Hamel & C.K.Prahalad (1994), Competing for the Future, Harvard Press

8   Henry Mintzberg & Joseph Lampel 'Reflecting on the Strategy Process', Sloan Management Review vol 40, no 3, Spring 1999

9   Gary Hamel 'Strategy Innovation and the Quest for Value', Sloan Management Review vol 39, no 2, Winter 1992

10 Rosabeth Moss Kanter (1988), The Change Masters, Unwin

11 Rosabeth Moss Kanter (1989), When Giants Learn to Dance, Routledge

12 Joseph O'Connor & John Seymour (1990), Introducing NLP, Mandala

13 Robert S. Kaplan & David P. Norton 'Putting the Balanced Scorecard to Work', Harvard Business Review, September–October 1993

14 Jim Collins 'Turning Goals into Results', Harvard Business Review, July–August 1999

Appetiser

CHAPTER EIGHT

In this chapter, you will:

- **FIND OUT WAYS TO EVALUATE YOUR SUCCESS AS A LEADER**

- **CHECK OUT YOUR PERFORMANCE AGAINST THE BENCHMARKS OF THE SEVEN LEADERSHIP COMPETENCIES**

- **EXPLORE YOUR PERFORMANCE IN EACH OF THE SEVEN LEADERSHIP COMPETENCE AREAS**

- **DEVELOP AN AWARENESS OF WHAT IT MEANS TO BE 'BEYOND WORLD CLASS'**

- **LEARN HOW TO CREATE YOUR OWN LEADERSHIP SCORECARD**

- **BEGIN TO REALISE THAT THE SECRET OF EFFECTIVE CHANGE LEADERSHIP IS THE ABILITY TO WIN HEARTS AND MINDS AND HARNESS THE POWER OF YOUR WORKFORCE IN ORDER TO WORK TOGETHER TO CREATE A BETTER FUTURE.**

Evaluating Success: Putting it into Practice

How does a leader know if she or he is successful? For any practising or aspiring leader this has to be the fundamental question that needs to be answered, in all its aspects. Human beings need feedback on their behaviour to compare the results they are actually producing with those intended. It has often been said that there is no such thing as failure where human behaviour is concerned. We are always successful at producing a result even if that result is not the intended one! In this chapter we are going to consider some practical tools to enable leaders at all levels to evaluate their performance and, as a result, improve their effectiveness.

We have to make it clear from the outset that there is no single questionnaire or measurement technique to evaluate leadership effectively in all situations. What we have done is to propose a set of tools, some or all of which might be suitable for the reader's particular position. None of these tools is better than any other, it is simply a matter of suitability and applicability.

To start the evaluation process, it is important to remind ourselves about the fundamental shift in the nature of leadership. We have already said that leadership has moved away from a focus on the individual and their characteristics towards an understanding of the processes they create. These processes involve operation at the strategic, operational and front-line levels. In Chapter Two when we explored the Key Drivers of Change, we suggested that for many leaders in the business and organisational worlds, it is possible to create a vision for the organisation in the form of a set of ten characteristics, the World Class Factors. In many respects, this approach reflected the traditional approach of task and relationship behaviour that has been an underlying theme in so many leadership models.

The seven Leadership Competencies

Before looking in more depth at the World Class Factors and their relationship with leadership processes, let us revisit the seven basic Leadership Competencies of Chapter Three: setting a direction, setting an example, effective communication, creating alignment, bringing the best out of people, acting as a change agent and decision-making in crisis or uncertainty. We can build a very effective self-evaluation tool around this set of competencies.

How good are you at the following in your day-to-day operations? Give yourself a mark out of 10 for each of the issues in Table 8.1.

Tabel 8.1 Evaluating the seven Leadership Competencies

1. Setting a clear direction by having a vision of the future, a strategy for bringing that vision into reality and a set of values of what is important in terms of how you run the business. _____

2. Setting an example in terms of how you personally operate on a daily basis in terms of time management, focus on priorities, coping with pressure and dealing effectively with customers. _____

3. Communicating effectively with both staff and customers. For example, how often do you brief everybody in your team about what is happening? _____

4. Have you managed to 'fire up' your team so that everybody is committed to the business in terms of making it successful? _____

5. Have you created a plan for each person in the business in terms of developing the knowledge, skills, attitudes and competencies they need to possess in order to work effectively both now and in the future? _____

6. Do you actively pursue a continuous performance improvement programme to identify better ways of doing things and then follow through with the changes? _____

7. How well do you cope with a crisis? For example, do you try to solve everything yourself or do you try to delegate the problem where possible? _____

TOTAL SCORE OUT OF 70

THIS IS BASED ON THE SEVEN LEADERSHIP COMPETENCIES PUBLISHED IN *THE BUSINESS OF LEADERSHIP* (Hooper and Potter, Ashgate 1997)

This questionnaire is a useful starting point for leadership assessment. However, one of the problems we have found in practice is that each of the seven competence areas is complex in its own right and difficult to assess fully with just one answer. For example, question 1 on setting direction breaks down into four areas: creating the direction, having a vision, bringing the vision into reality and operating to a set of values. We have addressed this issue by taking each of the seven competence areas in turn and creating a set of ten questions to probe each in turn. The first of these questionnaires is about the sense of direction issue (see Table 8.2a).

Assessing leadership skill

Give yourself a mark out of 10 for each of the elements listed in Table 8.2a.

Table 8.2a Creating a sense of direction – self-assessment

1. I have a clear vision of the future in terms of
   what I am trying to achieve as a leader. _____

2. I have clear strategies for bringing that vision
   into reality. _____

3. I have clearly defined goals with timescales which
   will enable those strategic plans to be fulfilled. _____

4. I am clearly focused on my key result areas and
   prioritise my work effectively, based on what I
   believe is important in terms of values. _____

5. My strategic efforts take into account the changes
   in the external business environment. _____

6. My strategic efforts take into account the internal
   environment and culture of my organisation. _____

7. My strategies take into account all three levels
   within the organisation: strategic, operational
   and front-line. _____

8. I balance both business and human issues when I
   create my strategic plans for the future and my
   decisions are based on a consistent set of a values. _____

9. My strategies involve creating a clear identity for
   my organisation so that it is differentiated from
   similar organisations and competitors. _____

10. In creating my strategies, I listen to a variety of
    viewpoints and opinions before making up
    my mind on the direction to pursue. _____

This questionnaire probes ten key areas of the leader's performance from the leader's self-perception of their operation. The value of the questionnaire can be greatly increased by having the leader's performance assessed by other individuals and this provides the basis for 360-degree assessment. We can thus convert this questionnaire into the 'others' perception' format (Table 8.2b) which will then allow the leader's operation to be assessed by the people who report to them in the organisation, their peers and the individual to whom they report.

Thinking about ....'s leadership, give him/her a mark out of 10 for each of the items listed in Table 8.2b.

Figure 8.2b Creating a sense of direction – others' assessment

1. She/he has a clear vision of the future in terms of what she/he is trying to achieve as a leader. _____

2. She/he has clear strategies for bringing that vision into reality. _____

3. She/he has clearly defined goals with timescales which will enable those strategic plans to be fulfilled. _____

4. She/he is clearly focused on key result areas and prioritises work effectively, based on what they believe is important in terms of values. _____

5. Her/his strategic efforts take into account the changes in the external business environment. _____

6. Her/his strategic efforts take into account the internal environment and culture of the organisation. _____

7. Her/his strategies take into account all three levels within the organisation: strategic, operational and front-line. _____

8. She/he balances both business and human issues when she/he creates strategic plans for the future and their decisions are based on a consistent set of a values. _____

9. Their strategies involve creating a clear identity for the organisation so that it is differentiated from similar organisations and competitors. _____

10. In creating their strategies, they listen to a variety of viewpoints and opinions before making up their mind on the direction to pursue. _____

Setting an example

Values-based leadership is increasingly being recognised by many writers as fundamental to the success of leaders in all types of organisation. By values-based leadership we mean that there is an unequivocal statement of what is important with regard to the way the organisation conducts its business.

Values are one of the core aspects of all types of organisation in that they should set a blueprint for how the organisation takes decisions. If an organisation states publicly that its people are its most important resource and asset and then responds to a downturn in business by immediately making people redundant, it puts the credibility of its entire value set in jeopardy.

What we have found in our research into organisations where values-based leadership is practised is that leaders set a good example and 'walk the talk'. They do not say one thing and do another for the sake of expediency. They live their values on a daily basis and this is what frequently underlies their success. Leadership is as much about behaviour as it is about rhetoric. People copy what they see their leaders actually doing in the way of behaviour rather than what they are told to do in explicit terms. This is our second dimension of leader competence.

So how good an example do YOU set? Complete the questionnaire in Table 8.3a and see how you shape up in terms of being a role model.

Give yourself a mark out of 10 for each of the elements listed.

Table 8.3a Setting an example – self-perception

1. I always try to behave in a way I want others to behave. _____

2. I often find myself coaching others in how to handle problem issues. _____

3. Other people tend to copy the way I set about tackling projects. _____

4. My personal standards are high. _____

5. Other people look to me for guidance on how to handle difficult interpersonal situations. _____

6. It is noticeable that other people tend to copy my management style. _____

7. I would be happy for other people to deal with me the way I deal with them. _____

8. I believe role models are important in terms of creating effective organisational behaviour. _____

9. I would not expect someone else to do something I would not be prepared to do myself. _____

10. Managers and leaders should always behave the way they want others to behave. _____

So how do your followers perceive the way you act as an example?

We can convert the questionnaire to the format for the leader to be assessed by her or his colleagues (Table 8.3b). Thinking about ....'s leadership.

Table 8.3b Setting an example – others' perception	
1.	They always try to behave in a way they want others to behave.	_____
2.	They often seem to be coaching others in how to handle problem issues.	_____
3.	Other people tend to copy the way they set about tackling projects.	_____
4.	Their personal standards are high.	_____
5.	Other people look to them for guidance on how to handle difficult interpersonal situations.	_____
6.	It is noticeable that other people tend to copy their management style.	_____
7.	They would be happy for other people to deal with them the way they deal with other people.	_____
8.	They believe role models are important in terms of creating effective organisational behaviour.	_____
9.	They would not expect someone else to do something they would not be prepared to do themselves.	_____
10.	They believe managers and leaders should always behave the way they want others to behave.	_____

Effective communication

Our third area of competence relates to communication. Give yourself a mark out of 10 for each of the elements listed in Table 8.4a.

Table 8.4a Effective communication – self-perception

1. I communicate my strategies clearly and in a way
    that other people can understand them.   _____

2. I am a good listener.   _____

3. I frequently call together groups of managers in
    my organisation to discuss various issues informally.   _____

4. I have in place mechanisms within my
    organisation to enable people at all levels to
    communicate their concerns on both specific
    and general work issues.   _____

5. I am just as happy talking to a large group of people
    as I am communicating on a one-to-one basis.   _____

6. I regularly talk to front-line people to find out their
    views on current issues.   _____

7. I am comfortable dealing with the media,
    including radio and television interviews.   _____

8. People at all levels in the organisation find it
    easy to talk with me.   _____

9. I actively seek out opportunities to talk about
    my vision and strategy.   _____

10. I use a variety of methods to stay in touch with
    my colleagues, including personal e-mail.   _____

And now for the other people's feedback on communication. Give.......................a mark out of 10 for each of the elements listed in Table 8.4b.

Table 8.4b Effective communication – others' perception

1. They communicate their strategies clearly and in a way that other people can understand them.   _____

2. They are a good listener.   _____

3. They frequently call together groups of managers in their organisation to discuss various issues informally.   _____

4. They have in place mechanisms within their organisation to enable people at all levels to communicate their concerns on both specific and general work issues.   _____

5. They are just as happy talking to a large group of people as they are communicating on a one-to-one basis.   _____

6. They regularly talk to front-line people to find out their views on current issues.   _____

7. They are comfortable dealing with the media, including radio and television interviews.   _____

8. People at all levels in the organisation find it easy to talk with them.   _____

9. They actively seek out opportunities to talk about their vision and strategy.   _____

10. They use a variety of methods to stay in touch with their colleagues, including personal e-mail.   _____

Our fourth area of leadership competence relates to creating alignment (see Table 8.5a). This is where the leader operates in such a way as to mobilise everyone's energy to work towards bringing the vision into reality. However, it is important to realise that alignment is not like cloning. Emotional alignment is about agreement on the vision, the purpose and the value set. At the same time, it is important to acknowledge differences of opinion because they can add to the richness of the operation of the organisation and the levels of innovation and creativity.

Give yourself a mark out of 10 for each statement.

Table 8.5a Creating alignment – self-perception	
1.	I use my energy effectively on a daily basis.	_____
2.	I encourage other people to use their energy in a constructive way on a daily basis.	_____
3.	I believe most people in my organisation are pulling in the same direction as I am.	_____
4.	Throughout the organisation, people have a clear view of my vision for the future of the organisation.	_____
5.	I have created a strong sense of common purpose in the organisation.	_____
6.	I do not tolerate or encourage departmental politics in my organisation.	_____
7.	There are very few people in the organisation who are 'out of tune' with our sense of direction.	_____
8.	Most people in the organisation share my enthusiasm for bringing our vision into reality.	_____
9.	People share my good feelings about working in this organisation.	_____
10.	I have created a strong sense of identity and cohesiveness in the organisation.	_____

And now for the other people's perceptions of your ability to create emotional alignment (see Table 8.5b).

Thinking about how..............................gets people in the organisation to work together, give them a mark out of 10 for each of the following items.

Table 8.5b Creating alignment – others' perception

1.   They use their energy effectively on a daily basis. _____

2.   They encourage other people to use their energy
     in a constructive way on a daily basis. _____

3.   They manage to get most people in the organisation
     to pull in the same direction as they are pulling. _____

4.   Throughout the organisation, people have a clear
     view of their vision for the future of the
     organisation. _____

5.   They have created a strong sense of common
     purpose in the organisation. _____

6.   They do not tolerate or encourage departmental
     politics in the organisation. _____

7.   There are very few people in the organisation
     who are 'out of tune' with their sense of direction. _____

8.   Most people in the organisation share their
     enthusiasm for bringing their vision into reality. _____

9.   People share ....'s good feelings about
     working in this organisation. _____

10. They have created a strong sense of identity and
     cohesiveness in the organisation. _____

Our next leadership competence relates to bringing the best out of people. Rate your ability with a mark out of 10 for each of the items listed in Table 8.6a.

Table 8.6a Bringing out the best in people – self-perception

1. I believe that everyone has great untapped potential in terms of their possible contribution to the organisation's success. _____

2. I encourage all managers to create individual development plans for their people. _____

3. I spend a considerable amount of time coaching the people who report to me. _____

4. I actively support ongoing appraisal on a regular basis as part of effective management. _____

5. I believe that people fundamentally want to be successful at their work and I do everything I can to help them achieve that success. _____

6. I see training and development as an investment rather than a cost. _____

7. I praise people regularly when they have achieved good results. _____

8. I focus on developing people's strengths rather than correcting their weaknesses. _____

9. I encourage people to talk about their training and development needs and actively support their personal development. _____

10. I look on our people as an investment in intellectual capital and am constantly seeking ways to grow that capital base. _____

Once again, we obtain other people's perceptions on the leader's ability to bring out the best in people (see Table 8.6b).

Table 8.6b Bringing out the best in people – others' perception

1. They display the belief that everyone has great untapped potential in terms of their possible contribution to the organisation's success. _____

2. They encourage all managers to create individual development plans for their people. _____

3. They spend a considerable amount of time coaching the people who report to them. _____

4. They actively support ongoing appraisal on a regular basis as part of effective management. _____

5. They display the belief that people fundamentally want to be successful at their work and they do everything they can to help them achieve that success. _____

6. They display the belief that training and development is an investment rather than a cost. _____

7. They praise people regularly when they have achieved good results. _____

8. They focus on developing people's strengths rather than correcting their weaknesses. _____

9. They encourage people to talk about their training and development needs and actively support their personal development. _____

10. They look on their people as an investment in intellectual capital and are constantly seeking ways to grow that capital base. _____

One of the fundamental issues we are addressing with this book is the leader as a change agent. Thus it is important that we now try to gain some form of assessment on whether that competence is displayed by the leader. Give yourself marks out of 10 for each of the following items listed in Table 8.7a

Table 8.7a Acting as a change agent – self-perception

1. When implementing a change I always make sure
    that everyone understands the reasons behind
    the change.   _____

2. I understand that individuals react differently
    to change and I take those differences into account
    with how I implement the change.   _____

3. I am constantly looking for new ways to
    improve the way we operate.   _____

4. I am proactive rather than reactive in terms
    of dealing with external changes that affect
    the organisation.   _____

5. I look on change as an exciting challenge rather
    than a threat to the *status quo*.   _____

6. I try to manage the amount of change with
    which we have to deal so as not to overload
    people or undermine their confidence.   _____

7. I am not afraid to challenge 'sacred cows' in
    the organisation.   _____

8. I understand that change frequently creates
    winners and losers and I take special care to
    ensure that the losers are looked after.   _____

9. I ensure that change is undertaken for sound
    reasons rather than for the sake of appearances.   _____

10. I always give people the opportunity to air their
    views on an impending change.   _____

Now we consider the other people's perceptions of the leader as change
agent. Give ....marks out of 10 for each of the items listed in
Table 8.7b.

Table 8.7b Acting as a change agent – others' perception

1. When implementing a change they always make sure that everyone understands the reasons behind the change. _____

2. They seem to understand that individuals react differently to change and they take those differences into account with how they implement the change. _____

3. They are constantly looking for new ways to improve the way they and their people operate. _____

4. They are proactive rather than reactive in terms of dealing with external changes that affect the organisation. _____

5. They look on change as an exciting challenge rather than a threat to the status quo. _____

6. They try to manage the amount of change with which we have to deal so as not to overload people or undermine their confidence. _____

7. They are not afraid to challenge 'sacred cows' in the organisation. _____

8. They seem to understand that change frequently creates winners and losers and take special care to ensure that the losers are looked after. _____

9. They ensure that change is undertaken for sound reasons rather than for the sake of appearances. _____

10. They always give people the opportunity to air their views on an impending change. _____

Our final area of competence relates to decisions and action in crisis and uncertainty. In many respects, we feel this is an area that is often overlooked by many of the established leadership models yet, from our perspective, it is perhaps one of the most important issues for effective leadership. We can investigate this aspect of leadership ability with ten relevant issues as with the other competence areas (see Table 8.8a).

Table 8.8a Action in crisis or uncertainty – self-perception

1. I always keep my head in a crisis. _____

2. I look on 'difficult problems' situations as
    exciting and sources of learning. _____

3. I use a systematic approach to solving problems
    under pressure. _____

4. If possible I try to delegate the detail issues in a
    crisis to concentrate on the overview of the situation. _____

5. People look to me to sort things out in times
    of trouble. _____

6. In uncertain situations, I always focus on the
    important issues and operate according to my values. _____

7. I try to minimise uncertainty wherever possible. _____

8. Under pressure, I find it easy to focus on both
    details and the big picture of what is happening. _____

9. I always listen to other people's opinions in crisis
    situations and never reject new information
    because it does not fit with my ideas. _____

10. I am not prone to creating panic either in
    myself or in others. _____

And now we can adapt the questionnaire items for other people to give their opinions (see Table 8.8b). Thinking about how .... behaves in crisis or uncertain situations, award a mark out of 10 for each of the items listed.

Table 8.8b Action in crisis or uncertainty – others' perception

1. They always keep their head in a crisis. _____

2. They seem to look on 'difficult problems' situations
    as exciting and sources of learning. _____

3. They use a systematic approach to solving problems
    under pressure. _____

4. If possible they delegate the detail issues in a crisis
    to concentrate on the overview of the situation. _____

5. People look to them to sort things out in times
    of trouble. _____

6. In uncertain situations, they always focus on the
    important issues and operate according to
    their values. _____

7. They try to minimise uncertainty wherever possible. _____

8. Under pressure, they seem to focus on both
    details and the big picture of what is happening. _____

9. They always listen to other people's opinions in
    crisis situations and never reject new information
    because it does not fit with their ideas. _____

10. They are not prone to creating panic either in
    themself or in others. _____

With these seven competence areas, each investigated with ten question items, we have created a comprehensive methodology for considering leadership ability both on a personal basis and in terms of gaining feedback from others. The problem with this approach, as with many questionnaires, is the time taken to complete the items. We have taken this into account with our next approach to the evaluation of leadership performance.

So far, we have worked on the basic set of Seven Competencies and explored these in some detail. We expanded this to a fifteen-item questionnaire with a graphical display to look at differences in perception between how a leader thinks she or he is operating and how that operation is interpreted by other people, subordinates, peers and superiors within the organisational structure. The fifteen-item questionnaire is a more practical tool in some respects than the full version we have just discussed as it only involves fifteen questions rather than seventy. What is lost in terms of comprehensive data is made up for with willingness to complete the smaller questionnaire!

The questionnaire is shown in Appendix One in both self-assessment and others' assessment formats.

Questionnaire 1 takes the fifteen competence items and creates a self-evaluation tool. Questionnaire 2 is the form for the leader to be assessed by their colleagues. If a true 360-degree assessment is being used, then the colleagues should be the individual to whom the leader reports, at least one peer at the same level in the organisation and then several individuals who report directly to the leader.

Although there are many ways of plotting the data, one of the most convenient is to use a two-dimensional plot with the scale of 1 to 10 on the vertical axis and the fifteen score items on the horizontal axis. The graph sheet suggests how this might be arranged. The leader's own score might then be plotted as X whilst colleagues' scores might be shown as code numbers ringed in colour to differentiate between the peer, superior and subordinate positions within the organisation. This very simple way of plotting the data will provide the leader with an immediate picture of the extent to which he or she understands how behaviour is interpreted. For example, it is not uncommon for a leader to score themselves high with, say, 7 or 8 on item 2, whereas their subordinates might rate them with only 2 or 3 out of 10. As it has often been said, the meaning of a communication is the response you get, not what you intended to communicate!

This tool provides a graphical way of assessing leadership and can form the basis for open discussion to enable the leader to develop a more effective relationship with the people for whom he or she is responsible.

The World Class Profile

Having looked at the idea of basic leadership activity, it is now useful to consider a typical organisational vision that a business leader might create. If that vision is to create organisational excellence then the World Class Profile is a useful starting point. As a leadership assessment tool, the World Class Profile provides a useful way of obtaining both a snapshot in time of how the organisation is perceived, together with a coarse indication of the trend-lines in terms of whether the organisation is moving forwards, static or moving backwards. In Chapter Two, we introduced the basic World Class Profile.

If we now consider not just the ten characteristics of the world class organisation but also the impact of creating these factors, then we can develop this approach further and it leads to a very useful way of evaluating leader success.

We can expand the basic World Class Factors by clustering them in three main categories:

- business factors
- relationship factors
- emotional factors.

What we are doing is to reflect the idea of task, team and individual operation of the leader and expand that perception to include such factors as finance, emotional issues and relationships both internal and external. When we cluster the basic factors and expand them, we arrive at the following suggestions for organisational characteristics which we will call 'Beyond World Class'. These factors are as follows:

Business factors

- strategic focus
- financial competence
- sensitivity to the total environment
- quality of internal processes and continuous improvement
- embracing and managing change
- the effective use of technology for operations and knowledge management.

Relationship factors

- customer and client relationship management
- internal communication effectiveness in all directions
- effective cross-functional working
- creating effective teams which learn together
- thinking about the total business process rather than one's own particular job
- dealing effectively with all stakeholders.

Emotional factors

- creating a sense of inspirational leadership
- encouraging innovation and creativity
- developing people at all levels
- encouraging positive beliefs and attitudes
- living the stated organisational values on a day-to-day basis
- creating an environment where people gain real pleasure from their work.

These eighteen factors lead us to an overall assessment of the culture of the organisation. Whilst culture is defined in many ways, one of the most useful definitions is that it is a reflection of the way work and other issues are handled in the organisation, exemplified by the types of behaviour which are encouraged and rewarded. Leader behaviour is particularly important in this respect, as people tend to copy what they see rather than what they are told to do.

What we are now doing is to explore the composite leadership model which relates strategy, operations and front-line or team leadership to the culture of the organisation. Thus the questionnaire in Appendix Two relates to the Beyond World Class culture in that it explores leadership effectiveness in promoting a culture which supports the integration of the three levels of leadership.

Having explored the culture of the organisation, we are now in a position to suggest a comprehensive leadership evaluation tool which looks at the strategic, operational and front-line processes. This tool can be invaluable in providing an insight into the leadership challenges faced in a particular organisation. In some respects the idea is similar to that proposed by Kaplan and Norton in their Balanced Scorecard. What is interesting about the Balanced Scorecard principle is that it suggests that organisational performance should not be measured simply by financial indicators but that a range of measures (including customer perceptions, internal processes and the growth and innovation activity of the organisation) should be taken into consideration as well as the financial performance.

The Balanced Scorecard principle starts with creating the vision which in itself is a prime leadership function. The vision then leads to the creation of a set of strategies grouped in four clusters: finance, customers, internal processes and growth/innovation. Success in each of these clusters is then determined by performance as displayed by a set of key performance indicators (KPIs). These KPIs are created for each individual business and lead to a highly effective tailored performance profile. Thus they reflect successful leadership processes translated from the strategic through the operational and then to the front-line levels.

Towards creating a Balanced Scorecard approach to leadership evaluation

We can start to probe individual leadership performance in relation to the success of an organisation in a number of ways. For example the approach followed in Table 8.9 starts to involve the idea that organisational success is about a range of issues both hard and soft. It is not just about the numbers, but also about human and emotional issues.It is convenient to cluster these issues into four distinct areas to enable us to create a scorecard approach.

These areas are: strategy, culture creation, front-line impact and action in crisis and uncertainty. They lead us to the idea of creating four scorecards.

1. Choose the elements of strategy and planning that you believe are most crucial to the successful operation of YOUR organisation.
2. Think about the culture of the organisation you are creating. What do you want YOUR organisation to be like in terms of daily focus and behaviour?
3. What are the front-line measures in YOUR organisation that will demonstrate that your leadership has been effective?
4. How are crises and uncertainty handled in YOUR organisation? Is there contingency planning or does panic prevail?

The creation of a set of leadership scorecards is very closely linked to the particular organisation. In particular, the strategic intent, vision statement, culture and operating values are key to the creation of successful scorecards and these have to take into account the specific situation of the organisation concerned.

Summary

Leadership and change are in many ways synonymous. Leadership implies direction and progress towards a vision. The challenge is how to mobilise the

Table 8.9 Towards a leadership scorecard: a developmental approach to developing effective change leadership in the organisation.

How would you answer the following questions?	YES	PARTLY	NO
Is there a clear vision of the future which is shared by the top team of the organisation and which has been translated into a form which everyone in the organisation can buy into?	☐	☐	☐
Has this vision been translated into clearly defined strategies, each with goals and targets stated in SMART terms, that is, specific, measurable, attainable, realistic and time-bounded?	☐	☐	☐
Are there clear-cut strategies in the financial functions of the organisation?	☐	☐	☐
Are there clear-cut strategies for developing the relationships between the organisation and its customers, employees, shareholders, suppliers and other interested stakeholders?	☐	☐	☐
Are there clear strategies for continuous improvement in the way the business handles its internal processes?	☐	☐	☐
Is there a clear strategy for developing effective teamwork throughout the organisation?	☐	☐	☐
Is there a clear strategy for developing the intellectual knowledge base of the organisation by developing individuals throughout the organisation?	☐	☐	☐
Is there a strategy for developing creativity and innovation throughout the organisation?	☐	☐	☐
Is technology used to the best advantage in the organisation in terms of developing both the operations and the knowledge base of the organisation?	☐	☐	☐

hearts and minds of the followers to enable that process to take place effectively. At the same time, the contributions of the followers towards developing the process needs to be acknowledged.

We said earlier in the book that effective Change Leadership is based on five key aspects: creating understanding; communicating the reasons for change; releasing people's potential; setting a personal example and self-pacing. We also looked at the drivers for change as well as considering how to develop effective change strategies. All of this has been set against a background of other people's views about creating effective leadership in an environment of constant change. Some of these thoughts have come from commentators and academics, and some from practitioners who have learnt their craft through bitter experience. The one theme which has been common for all of them is that they have thought deeply about change leadership. They have applied their intellect.

In this final chapter we have suggested a number of ways to evaluate leadership success in both qualitative and quantitative terms. In doing this we have recognised that, just like any other skill, leadership needs to be evaluated against objective criteria in terms which are familiar to organisations – hence the idea of Leadership Competencies, and a Leadership Scorecard, as well as 'World Class Factors'. This evaluation has focused on three prime areas of operation: the business or task issues, relationship issues and the emotional aspects at the individual level.

Creating a passion for change by Intelligent Leadership is about working in all three areas simultaneously.

The 360-Degree Leadership Appraisal

THIS IS BASED ON THE SEVEN LEADERSHIP COMPETENCIES PUBLISHED IN *THE BUSINESS OF LEADERSHIP* (Hooper and Potter, Ashgate 1997)

© JOHN POTTER *AND ALAN* HOOPER MARCH 1999

INSTRUCTIONS FOR COMPLETION

For each of the fifteen leadership actions in Questionnaire 1, give yourself a mark out of 10 and then total the scores to give you a mark out of 150.

Then make several copies of Questionnaire 2 and distribute to your boss, at least one person on the same level as you in your organisation and at least three subordinates.

Then plot your scores on the graph sheet supplied. Use X to mark your rating of your actions and then a number with a circle around it to mark the scores that other people have given you. You might like to code the scores from your colleagues with red for your boss, blue for people on the same level and green for people who report to you.

Differences in how you see your operation as a leader and how other people see your operation are then clearly identified and can be the basis for discussion.

Look for items where there is a large difference between your perception of your operation and the perceptions of your colleagues. Notice also if you tend to overrate or underrate your performance compared to how others see you.

What can you now do differently to improve your performance as a leader?

QUESTIONNAIRE 1

A 360-DEGREE LEADERSHIP ASSESSMENT BASED ON THE SEVEN LEADERSHIP COMPETENCIES (SELF-ASSESSMENT)

How effective do you think you are at the following leadership actions in your day-to-day operation?

Give yourself a mark out of 10 for each of the following issues:

1. I have a clear vision of the future, a strategy for bringing that vision into reality and a set of values of what is important in terms of how we operate. _____

2. I communicate my vision, mission and values effectively to my team. _____

3. I set a good example in terms of how I personally operate on a daily basis in terms of time-management. _____

4. I focus on priorities and communicate those priorities well to my team. _____

5. I cope well with pressure. _____

6. I cope politely and effectively with customers, both internal and external. _____

7. I communicate effectively with my staff. _____

8. I regularly brief my team about what is happening in the business. _____

9. I regularly 'fire up' my team so that everybody is committed to the business in terms of making it successful. _____

10. I have created a plan for each person in my team in terms of developing the knowledge, skills, attitudes and competencies they need to possess in order to work effectively both now and in the future. _____

11. I actively pursue a continuous performance improvement programme to identify better ways of doing things. _____

12. I always follow through with good ideas for change. _____

13. I cope well in crisis situations. _____

14. I always ask others for their opinions before taking major decisions. _____

15. I always listen to other people's viewpoints. _____

TOTAL SCORE OUT OF 150

QUESTIONNAIRE 2

A 360-DEGREE LEADERSHIP ASSESSMENT BASED ON THE SEVEN LEADERSHIP COMPETENCIES (OTHER INDIVIDUALS' ASSESSMENT)

How effective do you think ....is at the following leadership actions in day-to-day operation?

Give the person a mark out of 10 for each of the following issues:

1. They have a clear vision of the future, a strategy for bringing that vision into reality and a set of values of what is important in terms of how we all operate. _____

2. They communicate my vision, mission and values effectively to their team. _____

3. They set a good example in terms of how they personally operate on a daily basis in terms of time management. _____

4. They focus on priorities and communicate those priorities well to their team. _____

5. They cope well with pressure. _____

6. They cope politely and effectively with customers, both internal and external. _____

7. They communicate effectively with their staff. _____

8. They regularly brief their team about what is happening in the business. _____

9. They regularly 'fire up' their team so that everybody is committed to the business in terms of making it successful. _____

10. They have created a plan for each person in their team in terms of developing the knowledge, skills, attitudes and competencies they need to possess in order to work effectively both now and in the future. _____

11. They actively pursue a continuous performance improvement programme to identify better ways of doing things. _____

12. They always follow through with good ideas for change. _____

13. They cope well in crisis situations. _____

14. They always ask others for their opinions before taking major decisions. _____

15. They always listen to other people's viewpoints. _____

TOTAL SCORE OUT OF 150

LEADERSHIP ACTIONS ANALYSIS SHEET GRAPH SHEET

(Use your own colour-coding system)

=SELF

=OTHER 1   = OTHER 2   = OTHER 3   = OTHER 4   = OTHER 5

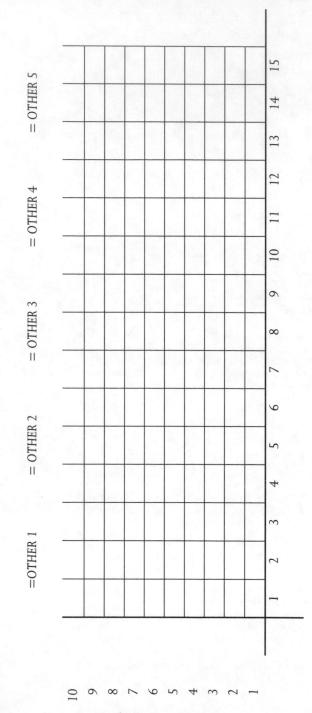

Beyond World Class: An Examination of an Enabling Corporate Culture

PART ONE – BUSINESS FACTORS	YES	PARTLY	NO
Have you a clearly defined strategic focus for your business?	☐	☐	☐
Are you well-organised in financial terms both in terms of day-to-day management procedures and long-term financial strategy?	☐	☐	☐
Do you monitor the changes in the environment in which your business operates?	☐	☐	☐
Are your internal processes constantly being reviewed and updated?	☐	☐	☐
Does the organisation actively grasp the challenge of change and overcome resistance?	☐	☐	☐
Is the use of technology for operational improvement and knowledge management encouraged?	☐	☐	☐

Score 3 for YES, 1 for PARTLY and 0 for NO.

TOTAL FOR BUSINESS FACTORS

Maximum score 18

PART TWO – RELATIONSHIP FACTORS	YES	PARTLY	NO
Does the organisation work hard to show its customers that it values their business?	☐	☐	☐
Are the internal communication processes within the organisation completely effective?	☐	☐	☐
Are there cross-functional teams which operate together effectively?	☐	☐	☐
Are teams encouraged to learn together by both on the job and off-site team-building activity?	☐	☐	☐
Do people think about how what they do if they make a change in the way they operate affects others in the organisation?	☐	☐	☐
Are the viewpoints of all stakeholders such as employees, shareholders, customers, suppliers and the local community taken into account when making major decisions which might affect them?	☐	☐	☐

Score 3 for YES, 1 for PARTLY and 0 for NO.

```
┌──────────┐
│          │
└──────────┘
```

TOTAL FOR RELATIONSHIP FACTORS

Maximum score 18

PART THREE – EMOTIONAL FACTORS	YES	PARTLY	NO
Do people in the organisation feel inspired by the leadership at the top?	☐	☐	☐
Is innovation and creativity encouraged by the organisation in such a way that people do not feel frightened to experiment and take appropriate risks?	☐	☐	☐
Is effort put into creating development plans for people at all levels in the organisation?	☐	☐	☐
Do people talk about the organisation in a positive way and display consistently high levels of motivation?	☐	☐	☐
Does the leadership behave on a daily basis in such a way as to reflect the stated values of the organisation?	☐	☐	☐
Do people enjoy and have fun working for the organisation?	☐	☐	☐

Score 3 for YES, 1 for PARTLY and 0 for NO.

TOTAL FOR EMOTIONAL FACTORS

Maximum score 18

Add together the three scores from the boxes and notice which is the strongest score and which is the lowest score. The lowest score gives the area to which most attention should be paid to create a shift towards a more positive culture.

Maximum possible score is 54
Scores above 45 are good
Scores below 20 require some serious consideration as to how the culture might be improved.

Bibliography

Adair, J.	*Effective Leadership*	Gower 1983
Adair, J.	*Training for Leadership*	Gower 1988
Adair, J.	*Great Leaders*	Talbot Adair Press 1989
Bass, B.M. and Avos, B.J.	'Developing Transformational Leadership – 1992 and beyond'	*Journal of European Training*, vol 14, no 5 pp21–7
Bass, B.M. and Stogdill, R.M.	*Handbook of Leadership*	New York: The Free Press 1990
Bennis, W. and Nanus, B.	*Leaders*	Harper & Row 1985
Bennis, W.	*On Becoming a Leader*	Arrow 1989
Blanchard, K. and Hersey, P.	*Organisational Behaviour*	Prentice-Hall 1969
Carnall, C.	*Managing Change in Organisations*	Prentice-Hall 1990
Carlzon, J.	*Moments of Truth*	HarperCollins 1987
Collins, J.	'Turning Goals into Results'	*Harvard Business Review,* July–August 1999
Conger, J.	'The Necessary Art of Persuasion'	*Harvard Business Review,* May–June 1998
Dixon, N.	*On the Psychology of Military Incompetence*	Jonathan Cape 1976
Edvinsson L. & Malone, M.S.	*Intellectual Capital*	Piatkus 1997
Fiedler, F. *et al.*	*Improving Leadership Effectiveness*	Wiley 1976
Festinger, L.	*A Theory of Cognitive Dissonance*	Row Petersen 1957
Garratt, R.	*The Fish Rots from the Head*	HarperCollins 1996
Geus, A. de	*The Living Company*	Nicholas Brealey 1999
Goldsmith, W. & Clutterbuck, D.	*The Winning Streak*	Penguin 1984
Goleman, D.	*Emotional Intelligence*	Bloomsbury 1996
Goleman, D.	*Working with Emotional Intelligence*	Bloomsbury 1998
Hamel, G. & Prahalad, C.K.	*Competing for the Future*	Harvard Press 1994
Hamel, G.	'Strategy Innovation & the Quest for Value'	*Sloan Management Review,* vol 39, no 2, Winter 1998
Hammer, M. & Champy, J.	*Re-engineering the Corporation*	Nicholas Brealey 1993
Handy, C.	*The Gods of Management*	Souvenir Press 1988
Handy, C.	*The Empty Raincoat*	Hutchinson 1994
Handy, C.	*Beyond Certainty*	Arrow Business Books 1996
Hartley, N.	*Towards a New Definition of Work*	RSA London 1996
Henley Centre, The	*2020 Vision*	Barclays Life 1998
Hooper A. & Potter, J.	*The Business of Leadership*	Ashgate 1997
Institute of Directors, London	*Sign of the Times*	IOD London 1998
Kakabadse, A. & Kakabadse, N.	*Essence of Leadership*	ITP 1999
Kaplan, R. & Norton, P.	'Putting the Balanced Scorecard to Work'	*Harvard Business Review,* September–October 1993
Kare-Silver, M. de	*Strategy in Crisis*	Macmillan 1997
Katzenbach, J. *et al.*	'The Myth of the Top Management Team'	*Harvard Business Review,* November–December 1997

Katzenbach, J. et al.	Real Change Leaders	Nicholas Brealey 1996
Katzenbach, J. & Santamaria J.A.	'Firing up the Front Line'	Harvard Business Review, May–June 1999
Kotter, J.	A Force for Change	The Free Press 1990
Mant, A.	Intelligent Leadership	Allen & Unwin 1997
Mintzberg, H. & Lampel, J.	'Reflecting on the Strategy Process'	Sloan Management Review, vol 40, no 3, Spring 1999
Moss Kanter, R.	The Change Masters	Unwin 1988
Moss Kanter, R.	When Giants Learn to Dance	Routledge 1989
O'Connor, J. and Seymour, J.	Introducing NLP	Mandala 1990
Pedler, M. et al.	The Learning Company	McGraw-Hill 1991
Peters, T.J. & Waterman, R.	In Search of Excellence	Harper & Row 1982
Peters, T.J.	Thriving on Chaos	Pan Books 1987
Platt, R.	Managing Change and Making it Stick	Fontana-Collins 1987
Pritchett, Price	New Work Habits	Pritchett & Associates 1994
Pritchett, Price & Pound, R.	A Survival Guide to the Stress of Organizational Change	Pritchett & Associates 1995
Rogers, C.	On Becoming a Person	Constable 1967
Ryback, D.	Putting Emotional Intelligence to Work	Butterworth-Heinemann 1998
Sadler, P.	Leadership	Kogan Page 1997
Scott, C.D. & Jaffe, D.T.	Managing Organisational Change	Kogan Page 1989
Schein, E.H.	Organisational Culture and Leadership	Jossey-Bass 1992
Senge, P.	The Fifth Discipline	Century Business 1990
Senge, P. et al.	The Fifth Discipline Fieldbook	Nicholas Brealey 1994
Senge, P. et al.	The Dance of Change	Nicholas Brealey 1999
Simons, R. & Davila, A.	'How High is your return on Management?'	Harvard Business Review, January–February 1998
Stogdill, R.	Handbook of Leadership	Macmillan 1974

Index

in uncertain world   150, 160
vision for   166
stress
    and age   120
    and capability   105, 106
    cost of   67
    quality of work under   15
    and under-stimulation   120
    in workplace   15, 103
    see also life events survey
success
    keys to   78–93
    measuring   167
'Survivor Syndrome'   5, 103
SWOT analysis   116–17, 151, 163

takeovers and mergers, change with   78
team
    culture   94, 96–7
    and individuals   107–8
    remote as leadership dilemma   65–6
    roles that make up (Belbin)   59
teamwork
    as basis for empowerment   140
    and hierarchy   46
    in public sector   97
    rewarding   97
technically-orientated training, emphasis on   22
'techno-fear'   *see* computer literacy
technology
    as driver of organisational change   32
    keeping pace with, resources required for   32
    miniaturisation in   32
    organisations embracing   15
    replacing people with   34
Thailand, shift from export-led to consumer-led in   33
Thatcher, Margaret   9
'thinking outside the box'   4
thought processes, left- and right-brain   166
Three Circle Approach to leadership   57
Total Quality Management (TQM)   41, 45–6
    failure rates of   45–6

Training Group Defence Agency (RAF)   81–2
training programmes   95
transparency   136
trust, building   136

values
    corporate   7, 38–40, **39**: as foundation of empowerment   90; management support of   7; for success **40**
    personal   104–6, **105**, 142
Volkswagen Group UK Ltd   73, 79–80, 91–2, **92**

Wagadon   87–9
wages differentials, East-West   33
'walking the talk'   7
water industry   156
Waterman, Robert   58
Watts Blake Bearne & Co   109
women
    in Japan and Thailand   3
    in work   6
work
    full-time   *see* full-time jobs
    as a 'good place to be'   46-7
    from home   6, 32
    socially stimulating environment of   32
    see also women; working hours
working days lost   15
working hours   6, 67
workload, managing, as leadership dilemma   67–8
workshops, size of   29
World Class Profile (authors')   42–8, **43**, 177–8, 195–8
    business factors   196, **209**
    emotional factors   196, 197, **211**
    relationship factors   196, **210**
    see also Beyond World Class; Leadership Competencies